W9-ACY-444

H. Wiley Hitchcock, editor

Prentice-Hall
History of Music Series

MUSIC IN THE MEDIEVAL WORLD, *Albert Seay*

RENAISSANCE MUSIC, *Joel Newman*

BAROQUE MUSIC, *Claude Palisca*

MUSIC IN THE CLASSIC PERIOD, *Reinhard G. Pauly*

NINETEENTH-CENTURY ROMANTICISM IN MUSIC, *Paul Revitt*

TWENTIETH-CENTURY MUSIC: AN INTRODUCTION , *Eric Salzman*

FOLK AND TRADITIONAL MUSIC OF THE WESTERN CONTINENTS, *Bruno Nettl*

MUSIC CULTURES OF THE PACIFIC, THE NEAR EAST, AND ASIA, *William P. Malm*

MUSIC IN THE UNITED STATES: A HISTORICAL INTRODUCTION, *H. Wiley Hitchcock*

Folk and Traditional Music of the Western Continents

BRUNO NETTL
University of Illinois

PRENTICE-HALL, INC., ENGLEWOOD CLIFFS, NEW JERSEY

for Gloria

Library of Congress Catalog Card Number: 65-17798

Printed in the United States of America
C-32288-C
C-32287-P

Current printing (last digit):
11 10 9 8 7 6 5 4 3 2

PRENTICE-HALL INTERNATIONAL, INC., *London*
PRENTICE-HALL OF AUSTRALIA, PTY., LTD., *Sydney*
PRENTICE-HALL OF CANADA, LTD., *Toronto*
PRENTICE-HALL OF INDIA (PRIVATE) LTD., *New Delhi*
PRENTICE-HALL OF JAPAN, INC., *Tokyo*

Foreword

Students and informed amateurs of the history of music have long needed a series of books that are comprehensive, authoritative, and engagingly written. They have needed books written by specialists—but specialists interested in communicating vividly. The Prentice-Hall History of Music Series aims at filling these needs.

Six books in the series present a panoramic view of the history of Western music, divided among the major historical periods—Medieval, Renaissance, Baroque, Classic, Romantic, and Contemporary. The rich yet neglected folk and traditional music of both hemispheres is discussed in two other books. The music of the United States, from the colonial period to the present, is the subject of yet another. Taken together, the nine volumes of the series are a

Foreword continued

distinctive and, we hope, distinguished contribution to the history of the music of the world's peoples. Each volume, moreover, may be read singly as a substantial account of the music of its period or area.

The authors of the series are scholars of national and international repute—musicologists, critics, and teachers of acknowledged stature in their respective fields of specialization. In their contributions to the Prentice-Hall History of Music Series their goal has been to present works of solid scholarship that are eminently readable, with significant insights into music as a part of the general intellectual and cultural life of man.

H. WILEY HITCHCOCK, *Editor*

Preface

Dividing the world into two halves for the purpose of investigating and discussing its traditional and folk or its so-called ethnic music is perhaps a dangerous proposition. But if such a division must be made, it seems logical to group together Europe, sub-Saharan Africa, and the Americas. These areas have during the last several centuries come greatly under the influence of Western civilization and its music—and they have influenced the Western high culture also—while the rest of the world appears to have been more under the aegis of the oriental high cultures. Moreover, in an American publication it seems perhaps appropriate to treat together those areas of the world which, broadly speaking, are responsible for the musical culture of the Americas today: Europe, Negro Africa, and

Preface continued

aboriginal America. Finally, the areas covered here can perhaps be thought to have produced about half of the world's music and musical styles, if such concepts can be quantified at all. On the other hand, there is not much unity but there is a tremendous variety of musical styles, values, functions, and instruments in the part of the world that is the subject of this volume.

Our approach is essentially geographic. After two chapters dealing with the general characteristics of traditional music and its cultural context, and with some of the methods used to study folk music, we devote four chapters to Europe, one to sub-Saharan Africa, and three to the Americas. It has been impossible, of course, to survey comprehensively the music of each area, nation, and tribe, and we must content ourselves with examples of the kinds of musical styles that are found, and with sampling the types of songs that are sung, the various uses to which music is put, and the plethora of instruments past and present. The musical examples are intended to illustrate points made in the text rather than to serve as a representative anthology of musical forms; but most of the things discussed are musically illustrated, and a few of the most important and unusual instruments are depicted.

I should like to express my thanks to the various publishers, collectors, and authors who have given permission to quote musical and textual material; individual credit is given with each quotation. I am indebted to William P. Malm for advice and criticism and for arranging to have the exquisite line drawings of instruments made by the prominent Japanese artist Masakazu Kuwata. I am also grateful to H. Wiley Hitchcock for advice and guidance and to my wife for technical assistance.

B.N.

Contents

I

Folk and Traditional Music in its Cultural Setting

Introduction

We are concerned here with a body of music called ethnic, folk, or "traditional," as it is found in Europe, most of Africa, and the Americas. This music consists essentially of two groups: 1) folk music, which is found in those areas in which there is also a development of urban, professionalized, cultivated classical music, and 2) primitive music, which is the music of the nonliterate cultures, those that do not have a tradition of sophisticated musical culture living alongside the musical folk culture. Although we really have no way of telling just what actually happened, we may perhaps assume that the musical development of all cultures was once something like the present-day folk and primitive music in the sense that it involved people who were not professional musicians, and that it consisted of music that all of the people in a culture could understand and in which many could participate. Then, among some peoples there must have taken place the development of a separate musical culture for the sophisticated segment of the population, while the unsophisticated segment held onto the old musical tradition. In our Western civilization we tend to be dominated by this sophisticated musical culture, and in spite of the proliferation of folk singing in our cities and on our campuses, we tend to know very little about the uncultivated, originally rural musical tradition in our own individual backgrounds.

We are concerned, then, with two kinds of music, the folk and the so-called primitive, which really—when they are first heard by the novice—have very little in common. European and American folk music is, after all, part of our own cultural tradition as members of Western culture. The traditional music of the American Indians and African Negroes is generally quite outside our experience. Moreover, each nation, each tribe, has its own music, and one kind of folk music may sound quite unlike another; Indian and African music are quite dissimilar, and Australian aboriginal music and the songs of the Micronesians are as different as two kinds of music can be. Our only justification for including such a large group of music in a single discussion is the fact that in each culture in the Western half of the world this is the music that is used by a large number of people. Our contemporary musicians usually tend to concentrate on the degree to which a piece of music is unique, and the complexity of its structure and texture, and they do not care particularly whether—in our classical music—the material is understood by many people, or by a professional few, or even by just the composer himself. Our interest in folk and traditional music revolves around the fact that here is music that is accepted by all or most of the people in a cultural group as their own. Of course the picture is not so simple everywhere. In some African tribes, professional musicians are indeed found, and different kinds of music exist for different groups of the population. In some Eastern European countries, certain songs are normally sung and heard only by men, and others only by women. We find that there is not the homogeneous mass of songs that early students of folklore sometimes envisioned for the simple community. And there are many borderline cases between folk and sophisticated music in all continents, especially those included in this volume. But the songs and instrumental pieces in folk and nonliterate cultures must be accepted by a substantial part of the population, otherwise they will not live. The reason for this is the way in which music is preserved and transmitted in these cultures, and this is done mainly by the process of oral tradition.

Oral tradition

In less technical language, oral tradition means simply that music (like stories, proverbs, riddles, methods of arts and crafts, and, indeed, all folklore) is passed on by word of mouth. Songs are learned by hearing; instrument making and playing are learned by watching. In a sophisticated culture, music is usually written down, and a piece conceived by a composer need never be performed at all during his lifetime; it can be discovered centuries later by a scholar and resurrected. But in a folk or a nonliterate culture, a song must be sung, remembered, and taught by one generation to the next. If this does not happen, it dies and is lost forever. Surely, then, a piece of folk music must in some way be representative of the musical taste and the aesthetic judgment of all those who know it and use it, rather than being simply the product of an individual, perhaps isolated creator.

As we've just indicated, a folk song must be accepted or it will be forgotten and die. There is also another alternative; if it is not accepted by its audience, it may be changed to fit the needs and desires of the people who perform and hear it. And since there is not, in the case of most folk music, a written standard version which people can consult, changes made over the years tend to become integral to the song. Of course this kind of change occurs for several reasons and at various levels.

Imagine, for instance, that a Kentucky or an Alpine mountaineer makes up a folk song—both melody and words. He may compose the melody by putting together snatches of other songs he knows, or simply by humming aimlessly while at work until he hits upon something that strikes his fancy, or again by systematically changing a melody he already knows. (We know very little about the way in which composing is done in folk and nonliterate cultures, just as we really know next to nothing about the mental processes involved in composing sophisticated music.) This man then teaches his song to his three sons. Son number one is a musical fellow who has a television set and occasionally goes to the city—hears more complicated music—and he, over the years, whittles away at the song, changing notes here and there, adding ornaments, and evening out the meter, until he has made very substantial changes which he would no doubt consider improvements. Son number two likes to sing, but has a poor musical memory. He forgets how the song begins, but remembers the second half of the tune. In his rendition, the song, which originally had four different musical phrases (ABCD), consists only of a repetition of the last two, and now has the form CDCD. This is what evidently happened in the case of an old English and American song, "The Pretty Mohea," which is often sung to a tune with the form AABA. The last two lines, repeated, seem to have become the tune of a popular hillbilly song, "On Top of Old Smoky." Son number three finally moves to Mexico, and while he likes to sing his father's song, he becomes so saturated with Mexican popular and folk music that his version of the song begins to sound like a Mexican folk song, with the peculiar kind of rhythmic and ornamental structure characteristic of that country's tradition. You can imagine what might happen at a family reunion: The three sons sing their three versions, and while a person who knew the old man and his song the way it was first sung would surely realize that the sons have sung three versions of the same song, a newcomer to the group would only be able to guess whether these three songs actually were descendants of the same original. Add a few generations, and one song has become a large number of variants. The original form is forgotten and can no longer be reconstructed from the later versions.

How does traditional music originate?

We have looked at the way in which folk music comes to us. Most of it is quite old, but it has changed. To be sure, new songs are made up in most cultures at all times. In some cultures, many new songs are composed every year or every generation, and in others, only a few new ones may appear in a century. But a great deal of the material, in all cases, is old, and thus we frequently hear about the great antiquity of folk and primitive music. But we must keep in mind the fact that this music, no matter how far back its roots, has probably undergone a great deal of change—because people wanted to improve it, because they forgot parts of it, or perhaps because they felt it necessary to make it sound like other music that they were hearing. Folk and primitive music, then, have for us the fascinating quality of being both old and contemporary, of being representative of a people's ancient traditions as well as an indicator of their current tastes. And they are simultaneously the product of individual composers and of the creativity of masses of people. This historical development—far more than the artistic merit of the individual composition, which may be considerable in the opinion of some, but which may also seem insignificant in comparison to Bach fugues and Brahms symphonies—is the main justification for a detailed consideration of traditional music on the part of sophisticated, urban students and musicians.

We have implied, then, that folk music is composed by individuals, but that subsequent to the original act of composition, many persons may make changes, thus in effect re-creating a song. This process, called "communal re-creation," is one of the things that distinguish folk music from other kinds. But the way in which folk music is created has not alway been recognized. Among the earlier definitions of folk music, that which stresses the anonymity of the creator is one of the most persistent. According to this definition, a song whose composer is unknown is a folk song. Of course there is a fallacy here; should our ignorance of the identity of a composer make such a difference in our classification of musics? Still there is some truth in this view, for the composers in European folk music and in most nonliterate cultures are indeed not known to scholars. Moreover, they are not usually known to the members of their own culture, and in most of the cultures with which we are concerned here it makes little difference just who makes up a song. There are exceptions, of course; in some Plains Indian tribes people remember very specifically who "made" a particular song, or who "dreamed" it (some tribes believe that songs come to people in dreams).

It was believed by some nineteenth-century scholars that folk songs were made up by people improvising in groups. Actually this is rare, if indeed it occurs at all. Controlled improvisation under the leadership of a music master does seem to occur here and there—in the gamelan orchestras of Java and Bali, for instance, and among the

Chopi of Southeast Africa. We have reports of American Negro slaves in the nineteenth century making up songs by calling to each other and gradually arriving at a song-like formula. But this kind of "communal creation" is rare. Nevertheless, those who formulated the theory that folk songs are the product of the communal mind were not unwise, for they must have realized the importance of the contributions of generations of singers, players, and listeners in determining the final (or is it ever really final?) form of the song. Of course, folk songs are normally composed by individuals, and in the case of Western European folk music, these may be professional composers, popular song writers, churchmen, and sometimes even the great masters of music. There are many instances of tunes from the classics–Schubert's "Linden Tree" and Papageno's aria from Mozart's "Magic Flute" come to mind–which have been taken over by the folk tradition.

The idea that folk music is closely associated with a people, a nation, or a culture and its characteristics has long been widely accepted. In some languages, the words for "folk music" and "national music" are the same. This popular notion is, of course, quite opposed to that which deems music a "universal language." Neither is really correct nor objective. Of course, it is possible to identify music as music, whether it is in a style known to us or not. Music is a universal phenomenon, but each culture does have its own, and learning to understand another culture's music is in many ways like learning a foreign language. No culture can claim a body of music as its own without admitting that it shares many characteristics and probably many compositions with other, neighboring cultures. Balancing the idea of traditional music as a national or regional phenomenon against the concept of folk music as a supranational kind of music is one of the fascinations of this field.

Folk music as national expression

At the root of the problem of uniting nation and musical style is the idea that a nation's folk music must somehow reflect the inner characteristics of that nation's culture, the essential aspects of its emotional life–its very self. This feeling has at times given rise, among the general population as well as among folk song scholars, to a rather politically nationalistic view of folk music. Unfortunately, folk music has at times been made the tool of aggressive and racist policies. This was to an extent the case in Nazi Germany, where the high quality of German music was extolled and the poorer stuff of the Slavic folk song was denigrated, and in the Soviet Union during the 1950's, when traditional folk tunes of all peoples, including the non-Slavic minorities in Soviet Asia, were fitted with words praising Stalin, collective farms, and the dictatorship of the proletariat. Of course, such use of folk music has no place in the world of scholarship.

But there is an element of truth in the notion that the folk music of a nation or a tribe has a special relationship to its culture. We have spoken of the need for general acceptance of a song if it is to be remembered. There are other points. For example, it seems likely that the general characteristics of a language, its stress patterns, its patterns of intonation, and of course the structure of its poetry, are reflected in the music of its people. Moreover, if we plotted the characteristics of the folk music of each people—the characteristics of its scales, its melodic movement, its rhythm, and so on—and if we fed this information, nation by nation, into a computer and examined the results statistically, we would problably find that no two peoples have identical characteristics, or identical styles of music. Thus, while each musical characteristic, by itself, would be present in the music of many peoples, each people has its own particular proportion and combination of musical traits and these interact in a unique way. Of course some musical styles are similar to each other while others diverge greatly. Thus we are right in believing that the character of a people's folk music is unique. On the other hand, it has been shown many times that melodies and songs travel from people to people. A tune may appear as a ballad in Germany, as a Christmas carol in Poland (in slightly different form), as a dance song in Slovakia, and so on. It is possible, of course, that the same tune was made up separately in each of these countries, but this is not likely. The more complex an idea or a cultural artifact is, the less likely is it that it was invented more than once by different people. And a song, even a very simple one, is, after all, a fairly complicated creation. Very likely the song found in several countries was simply taught by people on one side of the border to friends on the other side, or taught in many communities by a wandering minstrel. The tune could be easily learned, but the words were strange, could not be readily translated, thus were replaced by a poem in the language of the second country. But since the tune did not fit perfectly into the repertory of the second country, since it did not have the characteristics of that country's preferred musical style, it was gradually changed in ways that would make it conform. If the styles of country number one and country number two were tremendously different, the song would probably not take root at all in the second country but would be dropped. The various folk music styles of Europe are rather similar, and probably for this reason there are many tunes that spread from people to people until they pervade the entire continent. In contrast, when Spaniards and Englishmen settled North America, they did not absorb into their repertories many, or perhaps any, tunes of the American Indians, probably because these were too strange for absorption into their style.

We see that songs can be passed from culture to culture. The same is true, to an extent, of musical characteristics or, as we frequently call them, stylistic traits. A type of scale, a kind of rhythm, a way of singing can be passed from one people to another without a simultaneous passing of songs. If country number one has a particular kind of technique—say, for example, antiphony, the alternation between two groups, each singing a phrase at a time—that technique can be taken up by the people in country number two, who may impose this way of performing on their own songs. There is some evidence that this actually happened in North America. Antiphonal technique is highly developed in some African cultures, and when Africans came to America as slaves, some began living with certain Southeastern Indians, both as slaves and as refugees from slavery. The Indians, who had some singing in which a leader and a chorus alternated, seem to have started using particularly the African style of this technique in their own songs. It is obvious that in spite of the national or tribal identity of a folk music style, there is much sharing of songs and ways of performing music among the peoples of the world.

Another facet of the identification of people and music is the idea that each culture has a primordial musical style of its own, and that songs and traits that are learned at a later date in history are not properly part of that people's music. The key word here is "authenticity." An authentic song is thought to be one truly belonging to the people who sing it, one that really reflects their spirit and personality. Now it is assumed by some that each people or culture has only one kind of music, one musical style, which really fits its personality, and an authentic song would have to be a song with this character. Assuming that this is true, it would surely be difficult to decide which of the various musical styles used by a particular people is its true, authentic one. Nevertheless, such decisions have frequently been made by observers of folk song and folk culture. Often these decisions have been arbitrary; songs that sound simple or old have been labeled authentic, while those that remind us of Western popular music have not been accepted. No doubt each culture has had musical material that has been with it for some time, and other material that it has accepted recently or only partially, and there is justification for calling the former music authentic and for ascribing to it a special place in that people's heritage. But the close identification of one kind of music with each culture or nation is also related to a gross and widespread misconception, namely that simple cultures—folk and nonliterate cultures—are capable of learning only one kind of music.

Historical perspective

Such a view seems to deny a historical perspective. The great age of folk music is frequently stressed, though often it is not certain whether the age of individual songs or of musical styles is meant. But to assume that each people is, for all time, tied to one kind of music is to assume that no change has ever occurred in its tradition. This view we cannot accept, for we can observe change in the world's folk music traditions going on constantly. And while change may have been accelerated in recent times by the rapid Westernization of many non-Western cultures and by the growth of mass media, we cannot assume that change did not occur in the more distant past. After all, migrations of peoples have always taken place, cultural diffusion and acculturation have occurred at all times, and there is no reason to believe that peoples who have learned from each other to use the wheel, to construct instruments, and to smelt iron should have refrained from exchanging songs. It is rarely possible to reconstruct the music history of a culture through oral tradition alone, although we can find out something from the geographic distribution of songs and style elements throughout the world, from archeological investigation of instruments, and from the observation of change as it is occurring in the present. But the lack of evidence among, say, Hungarian peasants of an earlier kind of music than the parlando-rubato style would not allow us blandly to state that this style has been with the Hungarians from the dawn of human history. It is quite possible that the ancestors of these people learned and forgot various other kinds of music, either more or less complicated than that which they sing today. We can make no general statements about the history of folk music except that there must be a history, and that the kinds of changes in orally transmitted music are probably not too different from the kinds of changes that make up human history at large.

The foregoing paragraphs may give the impression that we reject the concept of authenticity outright. To be sure, there seems to be little to justify some of its implications. We are approaching the study of folk music with the assumption that we are studying the musical expression of many people. And we cannot neglect any aspect of this expression simply because it is not ancient, or because it was brought from the outside, or because it does not seem to reflect the personality of the culture. On the other hand, the concept of authenticity has its uses. We are, after all, interested in the musical expression of large numbers of people, and in forms that are acceptable to everybody in a tribe or a folk culture and which would be considered by such people as their own. This interest makes it necessary for us to omit consideration of much music usually called folk music. For example, we will not consider the arrangements of folk songs made by trained composers, great or minor, or by the folk singers of our campuses and cities. This kind of music, although it represents an interesting and aesthetically appealing development, is not relevant to our interests here because it is not the music of the whole folk culture. The songs may be the same in some cases, but the way they are sung is not.

Music as an aspect of culture

We are interested, then, in the music of a particular group of people. Those classified as nonliterate or tribal cultures can be defined with no great difficulty. Until recent times, for instance, there was no doubt that all American Indians were in this category. There were individual Indians who learned to read, and some became learned; some even became anthropologists who studied their own cultures. But the Indian languages had not been written down except under the stimulus of white missionary scholars, and in each Indian tribe, more or less all the people shared one kind of music. In the folk cultures of Europe and America it is more difficult to separate the folk music from the sophisticated, cultivated, or fine art of music. The distinction is a gradual one. The musical life of cities and courts, directed by trained, professional musicians with written music, is certainly different from that of the villages in which music is passed on by oral tradition and in which most of the people participate actively without much specialization. But some folk music exists in the cities, and some influence from the cities has always trickled down to the villages and at times inundated them. Everyone has a bit of folk heritage; on the other hand, the folk songs of most areas in Europe and America have undergone some influence from the sophisticated music of the cities. The popular music of the cities seems to occupy a sort of middle ground. We can draw no sharp line.

Much has been said about the differences between folk and art music as far as their use or functions in the culture are concerned. We frequently hear the statement that folk and primitive music are "functional," while art music is not, or less so. This would imply that folk and primitive music always accompany other activities in life, and that art music is always "art for art's sake." There is some truth in this distinction, but the over-all picture is a very complex one.

If we scrutinize the role of music in Western civilization, we find that music is not at all solely a giver of pleasure and a device for aesthetic edification. On the contrary, it is frequently designed to accompany activities of all sorts. We need to mention only church music, dance music, marching music, and the background music of drama, film, and television, as examples.

On the other hand, the ideal kind of music, the music generally considered as best and greatest by those most concerned with music, is the music designed primarily for hearing in recital or concert. Thus we would be right in stressing the role of music in Western civilization as being essentially one not involving other activities, but only because this is the idealized role of music, not because most music necessarily conforms to this image. And, to be sure, we generally respond by describing music as beautiful rather than judging its suitability for its particular function.

The converse picture is, on the whole, found in the folk and nonliterate cultures. We frequently hear that all folk music accompanies other activities, that it never fills a role of entertainment, that it does not provide simple enjoyment. Of course this is not the case; there are many examples, in European folklore, and in African and American Indian cultures, of music's being used as entertainment. Individual singers may entertain groups or themselves with music. In some African cultures, music is performed by professional or semiprofessional musicians to entertain political leaders or wealthy men. But generally speaking—and here there are great differences among the world's cultures—the traditional music is focused towards functionality. Songs are usually referred to not as beautiful, but as good or powerful, an indication that it is not the aesthetic quality of the song but the manner in which it fulfills its task (persuading the spirits, accompanying a dance, or giving an account of history) that is essential. Perhaps we would not be wrong in stating that the most significant musical creations in Western civilization are those which exist for listening only; while their counterparts in traditional music are those songs and pieces which are related to other activities and which fulfill their accompanying function in the most excellent manner.

Traditional music and art music

The way in which folk music comes about has fascinated students of this field. The question whether the folk creates or whether it only utilizes material created by a higher social stratum has frequently been asked. We have already stated that all music is composed by individuals. The old belief that folk music rises, like a mist, from the collective consciousness of the village or band is hardly worth an argument. But the source of the folk music is still a bone of contention. The nonliterate cultures, of course, must get their songs and the musical components of these songs from inside the tribe, or possibly from a neighboring tribe. It is sometimes argued that even the remote primitives have had contact with the high cultures of the world, and that they have derived their musical accomplishments by absorbing the music of the high culture, diluted though it may be by passing through tribes and nations. For example, it may be argued that the Indians of South America, some of whose music is exceedingly simple, in primordial times must have derived their style from that of China; and there are remote similarities to substantiate this theory. Certainly this does not apply to the everyday contact that exists between folk and art music in some European countries. In Europe, it is sometimes thought, both the songs and the style of music in each nation are derived from the same nation's art music. This idea, based on a theory, which is known by the German term *gesunkenes Kulturgut* (debased culture), assumes that the folk communities are inherently incapable of creating music —or literature, or art—and that they instead assimilate what trickles down to them from the sophisticated society of the cities. A time lag is assumed as well, so that the kind of style found in German art music in one century, for instance, is likely to turn up in the folk music a century later. No doubt there has been a great deal of influence bearing from the cities on the folk culture. We know of folk songs that had their origin in the city, and we know of sophisticated dances that became folk dances decades later. But we cannot accept the notion that all folk music is simply debased city culture. The evidence of folk song influencing the sophisticated composer—from Schubert and Liszt to Bartók and Enesco—is too great. Rather, let us accept a theory of mutual give-and-take to describe the relationship between folk and art music.

Defining folk music is not an easy task. Several criteria can be used, and each, applied alone, is unsatisfactory. The main one is the transmission by oral tradition. Folk music is not, in its native setting, written down. As a result it develops variants, and the original form of a folk song is rarely known. Folk music may originate anywhere, but it is normally created by untrained, nonprofessional musicians, and performed by singers and players with little or no theoretical background. Folk song is frequently old, and the style of folk music may be archaic. But folk and nonliterate cultures do have a music history; they allow their music to change, their compositions to be altered, and their repertory to be turned over. Folk music is frequently associated with other activities in life, but it also serves as entertainment. And most important, folk music is the musical expression of a whole people or tribe, or a significant portion of a culture; folk song must be performed and accepted in order to remain alive—which is, of course, due to our first characteristic, oral tradition.

Bibliography and discography

Introductions to the general nature of traditional music and its functions in society and as an aspect of human behavior are not numerous. Among the best are some of the articles in Funk and Wagnalls' *Standard Dictionary of Folklore, Mythology and Legend*, edited by Maria Leach (New York, 1949-1950), entitled "Song" (by George Herzog), "Dance" (by Gertrude P. Kurath), and "Oral Tradition" (by Charles Seeger). An overview of traditional musics, nation by nation, appears in *Grove's Dictionary of Music and Musicians*, 5th ed. (New York: St. Martin's Press, 1954), under the heading "Folk Music." A survey of non-Western music, especially in its historical perspective, appears in the first volume of *The New Oxford History of Music* (London: Oxford University Press, 1957). Alan P. Merriam, *The Anthropology of Music* (Evanston: Northwestern University Press, 1964), provides much material on the role of music in various nonliterate cultures.

Several scholarly periodicals specialize in non-Western and folk music; among them, we should note *Ethnomusicology* (Journal of the Society for Ethnomusicology); *Journal of the International Folk Music Council;* and *African Music*. Bruno Nettl, *Reference Materials in Ethnomusicology* (Detroit, Information Service, 1961) is a bibliographical guide to the whole field.

Some articles of interest that explore specific aspects of traditional music everywhere and which are relevant to points made in this chapter are Alan Lomax, "Folk Song Style," *American Anthropologist*, LXI (1959), 927-954; Maud Karpeles, "Some Reflections on Authenticity in Folk Music," *Journal of the International Folk Music Council*, III (1951), 10-16; and K. P. Wachsmann, "The Transplantation of Folk Music from one Social Environment to Another," *J-IFMC*, VI (1954), 41-45.

A number of records and record sets give examples of the music of many of the world's cultures. These are listed here, although they could also have been listed following Chapter 2 and in some cases later chapters: *Music of the World's Peoples*, ed. by Henry Cowell (4 albums) Folkways FE 4504-4507; *Primitive Music of the World*, ed. by Henry Cowell, Folkways FE 4581 (a smaller selection overlapping with the former); *Columbia World Library of Folk and Primitive Music*, compiled by Alan Lomax (over 20 records, partly reissues of older recordings, partly new material collected by Lomax and others); *The Demonstration Collection of E. M. von Hornbostel and the Berlin Phonogrammarchiv*, Folkways FE 4175 (reissue of an early collection that attempted to show the great variety of the world's musical styles); and *Man's Early Musical Instruments*, Folkways P 525.

2

Studying the Structure of Folk Music

Music of any sort, and folk music especially, should be examined in two ways: 1) for itself, its structure and its aesthetic effect, and 2) in its cultural context, its function and its relationship to other aspects of life. The second of these views has been briefly covered in Chapter 1. We have tried to show how folk music and the music of nonliterate cultures, as a unit, differ from other kinds of music as far as their origin, transmission, and cultural function are concerned. We should now like to devote some pages to the question of musical structure. In the subsequent chapters we shall examine various musics, continent by continent, from both of these viewpoints. But in order to talk about music we need to develop a vocabulary, and talking about or describing folk music and the music of non-Western cultures requires special adaptations of the technical vocabulary normally used for describing the music of Western civilization. Also, in order to distinguish the various styles of folk music throughout the world from each other, we should have some idea of what is common to all or most of these styles. Here, then, we wish to talk about the music itself, not about the use that is made of it, or about the words of the song, or about the instrument used to play it.

What actually can be said about a piece of music? We can say that we like or dislike it, and why; but this is largely a matter of opinion. It would make more sense to say how it is put together. This can be done in very complicated ways, and there are some published descriptions of music that defy understanding even by trained musicians. On the other hand, a layman with no background at all can, by listening and repeated listening, find out rather accurately how a piece of music is put together. In the case of folk music, which tends to be simpler than the sophisticated music of the trained composer, analysis made by listening rather than by examining a score is not too difficult. And the reader of these pages is advised to listen to records of folk music as much as possible, because understanding of music naturally comes much more easily through listening than from reading about it. Furthermore, while we can say a great deal about music with words there is also much that we cannot express.

Form

Perhaps the best way to begin analyzing a piece of music, either when one hears it or when one sees it written out, is to find the large subdivisions and the broad tendencies. Is the song made up of several large sections which contrast markedly? Are the sections of equal length? Does the tempo change considerably or suddenly in the course of the piece? Are any of the sections repeated? Or is the whole piece repeated several times? And if so, are the repetitions more or less exact, or are they variations of the first rendition? Do the sections correspond to sections or lines of the same length in the verbal text? These are the kinds of questions an intelligent listener might ask himself.

Simultaneously, we should watch for the arrangement of the performance, and this is especially important in studying music from a recording. We want to know whether the piece is performed by a single performer or a group, or whether there is alternation. Do several performers sing or play in unison, or does each have his own part? And so on.

Having identified the several sections of a piece, let us try to establish the relationship among them. One way to do this to give each of them a letter, and to repeat the letter when the section is repeated. When a section is a variation of a previous one, we would give it a superscript number: thus, A^1 is a variation of A. When a

EXAMPLE 2-1. German folk song, "O du lieber Augustin," learned by the author from oral tradition.

section is new but seems somewhat reminiscent of a previous one, we could indicate this by a superscript letter so that B^a is a section reminiscent of A. For example, the song in Example 2-1 could be

EXAMPLE 2-2. Hungarian folk song, from Zoltán Kodály, *Folk Music of Hungary* (London: Barrie and Rockliff, 1960), pp. 61-62.

analyzed with the following letters: $A^1A^2BA^2$. Sometimes the interrelationship is more complex, as in Example 2-2 where a section reappears at different pitch levels.

Example 2-2 could be analyzed by the letters $AA^1{}_5A^2{}_5A$, A_5 being a transposition, a perfect fifth higher, of A. Forms such as AABB, ABBA, and ABCA appear frequently in European folk music. In the music of some non-Western cultures, songs don't have a clearly marked ending. Some American Indian songs consist simply of a loose, informal alternation of two different phrases or sections of music. These can also be analyzed in terms of letters, as indicated here. The following Navaho Indian song (Example 2-3) consists essentially of two sections, A and B which appear in the following order: AABAAAB, and so forth.

EXAMPLE 2-3. Navaho Indian song, from Bruno Nettl, *North American Indian Musical Styles* (Philadelphia: Memoir 45 of the American Folklore Society, 1954), p. 47.

Listening to a sampling of records will soon convince the student that the various folk musics of the world don't have too much in common. To be sure, neighboring tribes and nations exhibit similarities, presumably because there has been contact between them for centuries. But among the more distant regions of the world there is vigorous contrast. Practically anything that could legitimately be considered music exists somewhere in the world's traditional cultures. Perhaps the only limitation is imposed by the need for transmitting the material orally (or aurally) without the use of notation. This makes necessary a certain degree of simplicity; and where some complexity exists, there is a need for certain unifying factors in the music which act as mnemonic devices. A drone (as in the lowest pipe of the bagpipes), the use of the same musical material in each voice of a part-song (as in a round or in polyphony consisting of parallel fifths), and the reappearance of a musical motif at different pitch levels throughout a song are devices that are arrived at unconsciously but which are eagerly accepted by the folk community, help the folk singer and his audience to organize the material in their minds, and clarify the structure for them.

Polyphony

Most of the music with which we deal in this volume is monophonic, which means that only a single tone is heard at a time, and there is no accompaniment except that of drums, rattles, or other percussive sound. But there is a good deal of European and American folk music, and a great deal of African music, that has more than one tone heard at a time, or more than one melody at a time, or perhaps accompaniment with chords. Several terms have been used to describe all of this music; perhaps the most satisfactory one is "polyphony," which we will use here to include all music that is not monophonic, whether it consists of a singer's own simple accompaniment with his guitar, or of a chorus, or of a group of different instruments playing a complex interrelationship as in chamber music. In a style of music that is strange to one's own ears it may be difficult to decide just what is going on in a polyphonic piece. Certainly there is not much point, when describing folk music from Russia or music from South Africa, in trying to apply labels used for Western music such as "organum," "fugue," "conductus," and the like, to music that developed quite outside Western European musical culture. One way to begin describing a polyphonic piece is to decide whether the various parts being sung or played at the same time are of equal importance, or whether one stands out as the leading or solo part. Then we could try to find out the melodic relationship among the parts. For example, do they use material based on the same tune or theme, or do they use more or less independent tunes? If the latter is the case, we could decide whether the relationship among the different voices or instruments produces imitation or canon (the most common manifestation of which is the round), the same tune performed at different time intervals; or parallelism, the same tune performed at the same time at different pitch levels; or heterophony, something like variations of the same tune played or sung simultaneously. At this point, also, we would like to know how much of the music is planned, and what aspects of it, if any, are improvised. Of course it would also be important to know what aspects of the music must be performed the way they are, and on what matters the performer would have had a choice and the right to make changes on the spur of the moment.

Rhythm and tempo

Moving to smaller units in the music, we can learn a good deal about the rhythm of a song or piece simply by listening. One way is to tap one's foot or clap hands in rhythm with the piece. We want to know, for example, whether the music is organized in measures that recur, more or less regularly, throughout, and where exceptions occur. This can be ascertained by the regular recurrence of stressed beats, or of louder taps or claps. We also want to know whether the drum or rattle accompaniment, if any, coincides with the rhythmic units of the melody. Then, quite aside from the meter, we could also describe rhythm in terms of the lengths of the notes found in a piece. This is something that cannot be found out quite so easily by listening, but which can be more easily described with the use of written notation. We want to know, for example, whether most of the notes are of one length—say, quarter notes—(as in Example 2-4, a North American Indian Peyote song), or whether perhaps there are notes of all sorts of lengths—from half notes to sixty-fourths.

The tempo of the piece is also relevant here. We want to know whether it is fast or slow, but our intuitive judgment cannot always be trusted. A piece that a Western listener considers fast (perhaps because of the speed of the drum accompaniment) may be considered slow by a person from the culture that produced it. One way to find an objective measure of tempo is to divide the number of notes in the melody by the number of minutes the piece takes; this would express the tempo in terms of average number of notes per minute.

EXAMPLE 2-4. Shoshone Indian Peyote song, from David P. McAllester, *Peyote Music* (New York: Viking Fund Publications in Anthropology no. 13, 1949), song no. 73. Reprinted by permission from David P. McAllester and Wenner-Genn Foundation for Anthropological Research.

Melody and scale

We come now to the aspect of music that has been of greatest interest to the serious students of music in folk and nonliterate cultures—melody; and this aspect is probably the most difficult to study or describe. A simple approach employs consideration of the melodic contour. We need to know whether the melody of a piece generally rises, falls, remains at the same level, proceeds in a curve, or moves in large leaps, and so on. Listening to the over-all movement of the tune is thus important. We are also interested in the ambit, or range, of a tune—that is, the distance, in pitch, between the highest and lowest tones. This can be found with little difficulty by listening. Finally, we come to consideration of the scale.

The uninitiated listener of non-Western music, and even of the folk music of Eastern Europe and perhaps of some Western European folk music, is often struck by the curious, possibly unpleasant sound of some of it. It may sound out of tune to him, and he will have trouble reproducing the tones and intervals if he tries to sing it. Also, he will be unable to reproduce the tones correctly on a piano. The reason for this is that the tone system or scale of much non-Western music does not conform to the scales used in the music of Western civilization.

A scale may be defined as the pitches used in any particular piece of music such as a song. A tone system, on the other hand, is all the pitches used in a whole body of song or pieces in the same style. One way to describe a scale is to count the number of different pitches or tones that appear in it. From this kind of description are derived such terms as "pentatonic," which denotes a scale consisting of five tones; "tetratonic," a scale of four tones; "tritonic" (three tones); "hexatonic" (six); and "heptatonic" (seven). The tone system of Western European art music was, on the whole, heptatonic until the period just before 1900, the point at which the increase of chromaticism made it necessary to admit that twelve-tone scales began to be the rule. It is quite possible, however, to have pentatonic music that fits perfectly into the chromatic system of contemporary music; just play the black keys of the piano, and you have a common type of pentatonic scale. Thus the mere number of tones doesn't really determine the character of a scale to any great extent; and the reason for the curious sound of some non-Western music is not to be sought in the number of tones used. But counting the number of pitches is something the casual listener can do without much trouble if he is willing to listen several times to the same record.

The distance in pitch between the tones is probably a more important indicator of tonal character. Thus, we could have a pentatonic song that uses the scale A-B-D-E-G, and another one that uses the tones A-B♭-B-C-D. Each uses five tones, but one uses large intervals, the other very small ones. Of course the number of interval arrangements that can be found in folk music is almost infinite, but the listener can decide whether intervals he hears are, on the whole, large, small, or medium, and get an idea of the character of the scale that he is hearing. The peculiar sound of some non-Western music is due to the fact that some intervals do not coincide with those we expect to hear. They don't fit in with our system of notation, or with our fixed-pitch instruments such as the piano. There is nothing abnormal about these intervals or scales; nor is there anything especially normal or right about the ones that we are accustomed to. Each culture develops its own musical system, and the listener can easily get used to different systems and find each one sounding normal and in tune within its own style. It is like learning foreign languages.

In some cultures there are intervals smaller than the half tone, that is, smaller than anything that can be produced on the piano. More commonly we find intervals intermediate in size between those used in the Western tempered system. Thus, the "neutral third," an interval found in various cultures, is halfway between a major and a minor third. Of course, in Western civilization we use several different pitch standards. The intervals on the piano are somewhat different from those produced on the violin. But we have a range within which an interval is considered "in tune." Although "A" is supposed to be 440 vibrations per second, a pitch of 435 or 445 would still, by most persons, be considered "A." Presumably a similar range of acceptability exists in the musical system—expressed, or unconsciously taken for granted—of each culture. And probably one may deviate from pitch more in some musical styles than in others and get away with it.

In many ways, the music of non-Western and some folk cultures sounds strange, confusing, and downright unacceptable to the uninitiated listener. There is a tendency in our earlier musical writings, and in the present-day remarks of the uninformed, to assume that this music has no structure and no laws, that it is improvised. The frequent tendency to label it "chant" indicates an assumption by such writers that the music is simply a vehicle for ceremonial words, and that it has little interest of its own. Nothing could be farther from the truth. The intricacy of much of this music—its consistent and logical structure—makes much of it a marvel of artistry. The simplicity is dictated by the fact that it must be memorized, and by the lack of notation available to the composer for the purpose of holding on to his ideas. Careful listening can, however, clear up much of the apparent confusion. Intervals that sound out of tune will not, once they are heard recurrently in several songs of one tribe, sound so harsh. Of course, all non-Western and folk music is not alike, so that learning one musical language, say that of the Plains Indians, does not by any means assure knowledge of another, such as West African. But as in learning languages, so in learning musical styles, each succeeding foreign style is easier to assimilate than the previous one.

Other aspects of music

A final point to consider in describing for oneself the music of a folk song is the tone quality and manner of singing. Although we have only very rudimentary terminology (words such as "harsh," "tense," "ornamented,") to deal with this important aspect of music, it is one of the most essential for distinguishing tribe from tribe and area from area, and one of the most immediately obvious to the listener. Moreover, most of the music of a culture is performed with the same tone color. Thus North American Plains Indians sing in a tense, harsh manner, while Bulgarians may sing with many trills, turns, grace notes, and other ornaments. It was thought, at one time, that each culture had a manner of singing that was biologically inherited. This now seems unlikely, but the theory is obviously related to the fact that even though a culture may have many different kinds of scales and rhythms, it is likely to have only one way of producing vocal sound, one manner of singing. (For a discussion of classification and methods of description for musical instruments, see William P. Malm's volume in this series, *Music Cultures of the Pacific, the Near East, and Asia*).

Description of a culture's music

Having described for ourselves one piece or song, we would like to describe the style of a whole body of music—all Sun Dance songs of one Plains Indian tribe, or all music of the Basongye tribe, or even the whole body of music in the Plains, or of one European folk culture such as the Rumanian. Of course, we cannot assume that all music in a culture will sound like the one example included on a record, or even that all songs of a given tribe exhibit some of the same characteristics. Nevertheless, we frequently hear statements such as "the Ibo have this kind of music" or "Spanish folk music sounds like that." Fortunately for the serious scholar in our field, there is a good deal of stylistic unity in the folk music of each culture. The unity is probably greatest in the world's simplest cultures and gives way to increasing diversity as the cultures get more complex. The description of the musical style of a whole culture is bound to be essentially a statistical statement. There are few traits of music that don't occur at least to a small degree in many cultures, but the extent to which they occur varies and is important. When we say, for example, that most of the scales of the Arapaho Indians are tetratonic, that is, they have four tones, we must add that there are also many songs with five or six tones, some with three, and a few with seven. When we say that English folk songs are essentially modal, which implies seven tones to the scale, we must realize that all sorts of other scales also appear. Of course, here again we come upon the problem of distinguishing among several kinds of music: the true, essential, integral music of a people, the recent imports and the results of outside influences, and the atypical creations which don't really belong. Or can we make this distinction?

In the other chapters of this survey, we will be describing musical styles—along with their cultural background. We should admit at the outset that we don't really know enough about the folk music of Europe, Africa, and the Americas to give a reliable description. Many songs have been collected, many recordings are available; but the job of analyzing the songs and of describing the styles in scholarly terms has actually just begun. The statements that will be made in this volume will sometimes have to be impressionistic, based on knowledge of only a segment of a people's music.

We can only indicate examples of the kinds of things that occur. We cannot give a complete picture, but we hope that the partial picture presented will stimulate the reader to strike out on his own in order to learn more.

Research in traditional music—ethnomusicology

Perhaps a few words about the way in which research in folk and non-Western music is done will help the reader to understand some of the procedures and statements in the following chapters.

The field that provides research in this area is now known as ethnomusicology. Before about 1950 it was commonly called comparative musicology, and it is a sort of borderline area between musicology (the study of all aspects of music in a scholarly fashion) and anthropology (the study of man, his culture, and especially the cultures outside the investigator's own background). Research in ethnomusicology consists essentially of two activities, field work and desk or laboratory work. In past decades it was customary to keep these activities quite distinct. Those who went into the "field," to villages, reservations, or colonies, to record, were not necessarily trained in the techniques of analysis and description that form the main part of the "desk work," and the armchair ethnomusicologists rarely went into the "field." More recently it has been found that better results are usually obtained if the same person does both the field and the desk work on a particular project.

Going into the field requires more than a tape recorder, a generator, and a tent. The person who goes off to record the music of an African tribe or a Balkan village must know, in advance, a good deal about the culture of the people he will visit. Once there, he must use certain techniques to be sure that he gains access to the individuals who know songs, and that he makes representative samplings of the music. He should not, for example, try to record only one kind of song. Thus, a collector of folk songs in the Virginia mountains should not try to record only old English ballads. If he does so, not only will he miss much other valuable material, but he may also alienate the singers, since they will probably consider other songs equally valuable; and in so doing he may not succeed in hearing even as many old English ballads as he would if he had taken a more broad-minded approach. He must get to know people in the community very well. A three-day field trip is usually not very successful; the ideal field work requires months and years of stay, with brief follow-up visits to see how songs have changed and how attitudes toward music have altered.

Turning on the recorder and getting on a tape all the music one can is only part of the job of a field collector. The cultural context of the music—the answers to the questions that we posed in Chapter 1—is equally important and more difficult to obtain. The field worker should find out what his informants think about the songs they sing, what they consider a good song or a bad one, and why; how they learn songs; how they compose; who the good musicians are, and what makes them good musicians; what kinds of songs the culture has (according to the tribe's own classification); what kinds of terms they use, if any, to talk about music; what kinds of music outside their own they have had contact with; what activities each song is designed to accompany, if any; what the status of the musician in the society is; and so on. The field worker may have to use special eliciting techniques. For example, David McAllester,[1] widely known for his collecting of Navaho music, says that he persuades the Indians to sing for him by singing folk songs or even Indian songs to them. It may be useful to find an informant who will assume the role of teacher to the field worker. It is necessary to record the same song as it is sung by different people in a community, or by the same person at different times, in order to find out what aspects of a song remain stable, which ones are subject to change by improvisation, and also how much a song changes in a given period of time. Thus, the task of the ethnomusicological field worker is a fascinating but certainly also a difficult one.

Transcription and analysis

Arriving back at his office with a collection, the ethnomusicologist must set about analyzing and describing the music. He may do this simply by listening, with techniques something like those described in the first pages of this chapter. More likely he will want to set at least some of his music down on paper, with notation. This process is called transcription.

Since our ordinary system of notation was devised essentially for the music of Western civilization, and since its purpose is to help a performer carry out the composer's intentions rather than to describe the musical actions of the performer, it is not surprising that the system is rather imperfect for the descriptive use to which it must be put in ethnomusicological transcription. The fact that the rhythms and scales of non-Western and folk music may not fit into the Western system makes it all the more difficult to reproduce the music of other cultures in conventional notation. Various special

[1] David P. McAllester, *Enemy Way Music* (Cambridge, Mass.: Peabody Museum of American Archaeology and Ethnology, Harvard University, 1954).

systems have been devised, but most scholars have returned to the conventional one despite its shortcomings. It is one, after all, that can be easily mastered, and that is already understood by individuals who are acquainted with music. It can be used in folk song collections that serve the double purpose of being scholarly descriptions of music and providing music to be performed. Some transcribers have added special symbols to help where the conventional system of notation does not provide a solution. For example, intervals smaller than half-steps are frequently indicated by placing a "plus" (higher) or a "minus" (lower) above a note.

But careful listening to even a simple folk tune indicates that a considerable number of minor musical events take place in every second of singing. The question is whether we should try to capture each of these or whether we should restrict our notation to the main lines. The ethnomusicologist, careful and thorough, would like to capture all. If he has a talented ear and enormous patience, he will come up with a very intricate notation that can hardly be deciphered without a magnifying glass. This procedure was followed by Béla Bartók, the great composer who was also one of the most important scholars of folk music, and who collected vast numbers of Hungarian, Slovak, Yugoslav, and Rumanian folk songs. Example 2-5 shows one of his transcriptions of Yugoslav folk music. Below the melody in all its detail is a less complicated version of the song that gives only the main notes.

Of course, the important thing in transcribing is to be objective, to write down what actually occurs and not what the transcriber, with his ear used to a particular musical idiom (usually the Western one), may think he hears. And make no mistake about this: What you hear is conditioned not only by what sound is actually produced, but also by what sound your mind is attuned to and expects. Consequently, transcribing is a process that requires hearing and rehearing a piece; a minute of music may take two hours to transcribe.

In order to save time and increase accuracy and objectivity, several attempts have been made to devise machinery that would measure pitch and transcribe music. These range from a monochord—simply one stretched string with a graduated table to show vibration rates—invented by Jaap Kunst, to elaborate electronic devices based on the oscilloscope. The latter exist mainly in three forms, one invented by Charles Seeger and used at U.C.L.A., another developed

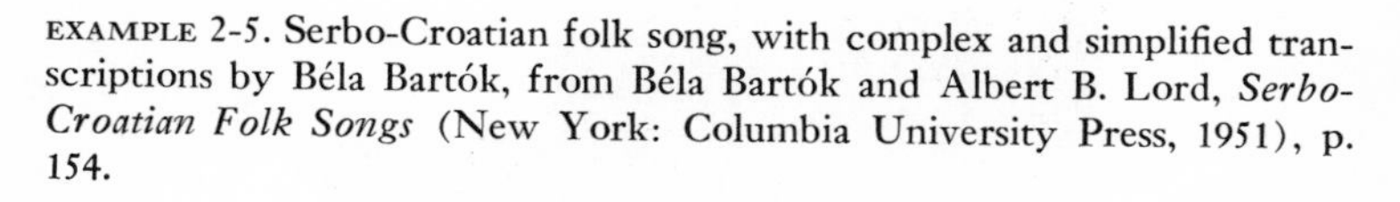

EXAMPLE 2-5. Serbo-Croatian folk song, with complex and simplified transcriptions by Béla Bartók, from Béla Bartók and Albert B. Lord, *Serbo-Croatian Folk Songs* (New York: Columbia University Press, 1951), p. 154.

in Israel, and a third invented by a group of Norwegian scholars headed by Olav Gurvin.[2] These machines produce detailed graphs which must be retranslated into something more meaningful than the sample in Example 2-6, usually into conventional notation, with all its faults. But electronic transcription does hold great promise for the future of research in traditional music.

[2] Charles Seeger, "Prescriptive and Descriptive Music Writing," *Musical Quarterly* LXIV (1958), 184-95. Karl Dahlback, *New Methods in Vocal Folk Music Research* (Oslo: Oslo University Press, 1958).

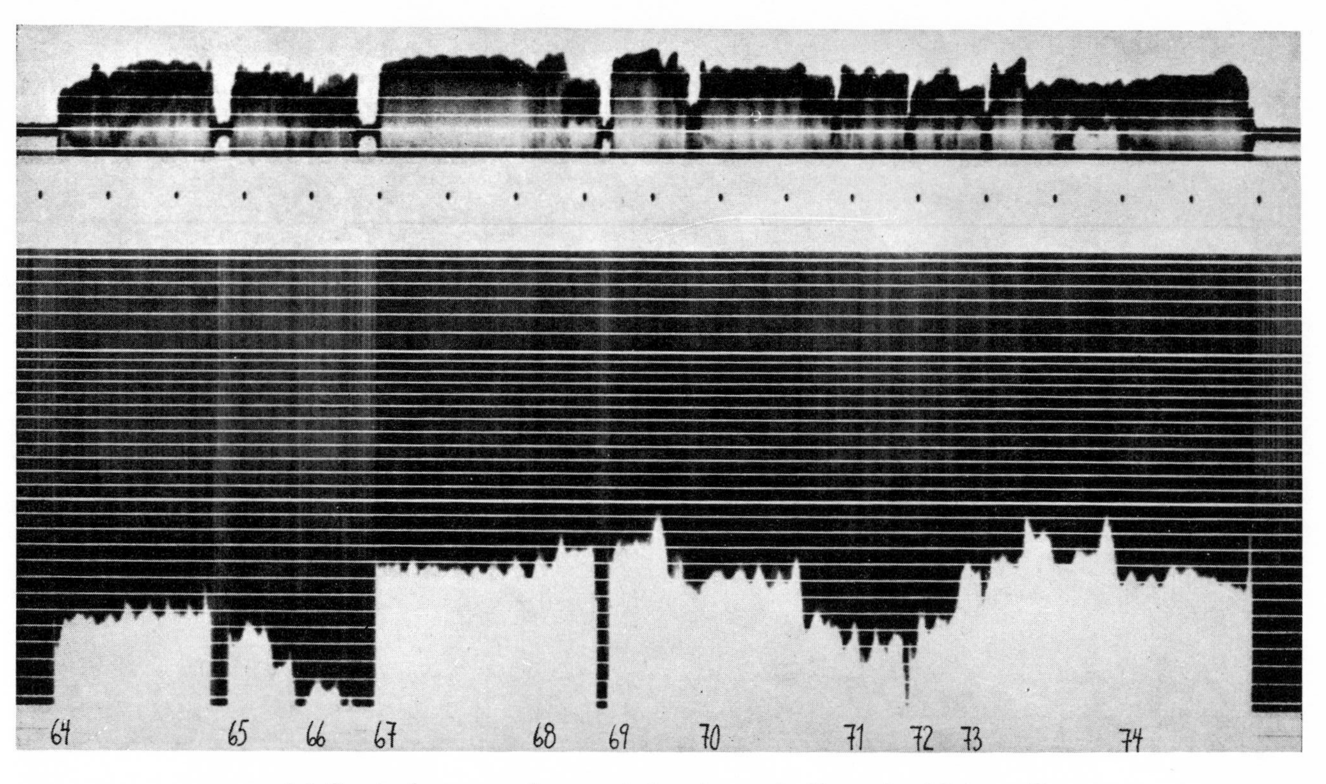

EXAMPLE 2-6. Graph of an automatic transcription of part of a Norwegian folk song. Top section indicates amplitude or rhythm, middle section the time, and bottom section, the pitch movement or melody; from Karl Dahlback, *New Methods in Vocal Folk Music Research* (Oslo: Oslo University Press, 1958), p. 127.

Following transcription come analysis and description of the musical styles and of the cultural background and context of the music. The kinds of problems that ethnomusicologists confront range from investigations into the history and the unrecorded prehistory of folk styles, the movement of music from one people to another, the interrelationship between the words and music of song, the history and structure of folk instruments, and the tribal aesthetics of music, to narrower and more intensive studies into the musical repertory of a single folk singer and the interrelationship of the variants of a single song. A few examples of such studies are mentioned in further chapters.

Bibliography

Methods of analysis and approaches to describing musical styles in their various phases are set forth in Curt Sachs, *The Wellsprings of Music* (The Hague: M. Nijhoff, 1962). Curt Sachs, *The Rise of Music in the Ancient World* (New York: Norton, 1943) also discusses the various elements of music and introduces the field of ethnomusicology. Many publications deal with methods of analyzing individual aspects of music. Among them we mention only Sirvart Poladian, "Melodic Contour in Traditional Music," *J-IFMC*, III (1951), 30-35; Mieczyslaw Kolinski, "Consonance and Dissonance," *Ethnomusicology*, VI (1962), 66-74; Kolinski, "Determinants of Tonal Construction in Tribal Music," *Musical Quarterly*, XLIII (1957), 50-56; and Curt Sachs, *Rhythm and Tempo* (New York: Norton, 1953), the first two chapters.

General works about the field of ethnomusicology, its history and theories, are Jaap Kunst, *Ethnomusicology*, 3rd ed. (The Hague: M. Nijhoff, 1959) and Bruno Nettl, *Theory and Method in Ethnomusicology* (New York: Free Press of Glencoe, Inc., 1964). Special developments of ethnomusicology in the U.S. are discussed in Mantle Hood, "Music, the Unknown" in *Musicology* (Englewood Cliffs, N.J.: Prentice-Hall, 1963). Other discussions of research methods appear in Alan P. Merriam, "Ethnomusicology, Discussion and Definition of the Field," *Ethnomusicology*, IV (1960), 107-14 and Willard Rhodes, "Towards a Definition of Ethnomusicology," *American Anthropologist*, LVIII (1956), 457-63. George Herzog, *Research in Primitive and Folk Music in the United States, A Survey* (Washington: A.C.L.S., 1936) gives information on archives and field collections. The standard work on instruments is Curt Sachs, *The History of Musical Instruments* (New York: Norton, 1940), and the basic book on dance, including that of non-Western cultures, is Curt Sachs, *A World History of the Dance* (New York: Norton, 1937). An excellent survey of recent research in non-Western dance is Gertrude P. Kurath, "Panorama of Dance Ethnology," *Current Anthropology*, I (1960), 233-54. *Ethnomusicology* VII (1964), 223-77 contains a detailed symposium on transcription and analysis on the basis of a single Bushman song.

3

The General Character of European Folk Music

"What is Europe? Is it an aggregate of separate cultures or an integral unit? And what is European folk song? A single body of music or simply a group of separate styles as large in number as the continent's nations and languages?" These questions are asked by Walter Wiora,[1] a leading authority on folk music, and they are good questions with which to begin a discussion of European folk music. Of course, a qualified "yes" can be said to each of these questions. In some ways, European folk music is indeed a single corpus of musical style. The various European folk musics have much in

[1] Walter Wiora, *Europäischer Volksgesang* (Cologne: Arno Volk Verlag, 1950), p. 5.

common, but each country—in some cases each region, each district, and each community—has its own music and its own style. In this chapter we would like to devote ourselves to exploring the unity of European folk music. In Chapters 4, 5, and 6 we will try to discuss the special characteristics of regions and countries.

We have pointed out that it is very hard to state concretely just how much difference there is between one kind or style of music and another. One way of telling that a musical style is similar to another one, the second of which you already recognize, is if the first of the styles also appeals to you. If this is true, and a person who is acquainted with British folk music finds Russian folk song more appealing than the music of Polynesia, then Russian and English folk song are indeed more similar to each other than are the English and the Polynesian. If we use this only very moderately reliable measuring device, we must admit that most of the European styles are rather similar to each other. And, on the whole, those that are geographically close to each other are also the most closely related in terms of musical style. There are a number of characteristics which we find to be present throughout Europe—with the usual pockets of exception, of course—and throughout that part of the world inhabited by descendants of Europeans.

We really know very little about the history of European folk song. We have little evidence as to the age of individual songs, although some idea can be gained from the notations of folk songs made by composers ever since the Renaissance. But in such cases we don't know whether a song was really part of the folk tradition, or whether it was an art or popular song that later moved into the realm of folklore—or vice versa. We also know little about the age of the various styles of folk music in Europe. Still, we are sure that for centuries there has been a close relationship between the art music of the continent and its folk music. How could it be otherwise? Neither villages nor cities live without some mutual contact. In the early Middle Ages, wandering minstrels carried their tunes from court to village and from country to country. The villagers of the Middle Ages attended church and heard Gregorian chant. The composer at the court of a minor duke in seventeenth-century Germany drew his performers from the village musicians living on his lord's estate. We have ample evidence for assuming a constant relationship between the folk musician and his sophisticated counterpart.

Of course the effect of art music on folk music is dependent on the existence of a well-developed fine-art tradition in music. Such a tradition evidently did not exist to a large degree before the Middle Ages, and it did not come to Eastern Europe until even later. There are those who believe that the styles of European folk music evolved to a state similar to what it is now before the time (perhaps a thousand years ago) when the sophisticated composers first began to influence folklore, that the folk styles are an invaluable remnant of precultivated times, even of prehistoric eras. This belief can be neither substantiated nor negated. But we are probably much safer in believing that the styles of European folk music developed some time in the Middle Ages, and that this happened to some extent under the influence of the art music that was also developing at the time. This, after all, might account for the rather considerable degree of homogeneity in European folk music.

The strophic form

The most characteristic trait of European folk songs is their strophic structure. We tend to accept an arrangement in which a tune with several lines is repeated several times, each time with different words, as normal. But this kind of arrangement is not so common elsewhere in the world, and it ties the European nations together as a musical unit. The length of a song with stanzas (called "strophic" song in technical terminology) can vary greatly, from a short bit such as that in Example 3-1 to a relatively elaborate piece such as that in Example 3-2.

The special character of the strophic song is derived from a peculiar trait of European poetry—folk poetry as well as that of the sophisticated poets. This is the tendency to arrange poems into units of two, three, four, five, six, or more lines. Such units, called stanzas or strophes, have a form that is repeated; the interrelationship of the lines is repeated, but the words—or at least most of them—are not. The lines may be interrelated by the number of syllables or of poetic feet per line, or, more commonly, by a rime scheme. But in any event, some sort of structure is given to the stanza quite aside from the meaning of the words. The words themselves, of course, progress throughout the poem, telling a story or expressing the poet's feelings

EXAMPLE 3-1. Slovak folk song with short stanza, learned by the author from oral tradition.

EXAMPLE 3-2. Irish folk song, "Patty McGinty's Goat," collected in Newfoundland by MacEdward Leach, transcribed by Bruno Nettl.

about practically any subject. But the structure of the stanza is repeated. We don't know, of course, whether such a strophic structure in the poetry came first, or whether it was invented to fit a song; this may be a case of the "chicken-and-egg" dilemma. But logically, it is a simple transition from a repeated poetic structure to a repeated melody, with the words and their content changing from stanza to stanza.

For example, the following stanza of the famous English ballad, "Barbara Allen," shows us some of the traits of the poetic unit typical in European folklore:

Oh yes I'm sick, I'm very sick
And death is in me dwelling;
No better, no better I ever shall be
If I can't have Barb'ry Allen.

Even if we saw the poem without music and without the printer's divisions into stanzas, we could easily figure out that it is arranged into stanzas, because: 1) lines 2 and 4 rime (also lines 6 and 8, lines 10 and 12, etc.), and 2) every fourth line ends with the words "Barb'ry Allen." In other songs, and in other languages, there are different characteristics of the stanza, different ways of identifying the stanza as a unit. But the same kind of musical structure, strophic, with its repetition of a few musical lines, is found throughout Europe (but not in all songs) and is simply an accompaniment and an analogue of the poetic structure.

The close relationship between the words and music of a song is carried even further in European folk song. The lines of music and text usually coincide, and the points at which the music comes to a temporary rest are also those at which a sentence, phrase, or thought in the words is completed. There is, moreover, a close relationship between the smaller segments of musical and linguistic structure, for example, between stress and accent, and between the length of tone and of syllable. The nature of this relationship varies from nation to nation because of the differences in structure among the various languages.

Characteristics of European scales

We have already mentioned the basic strophic structures as a reason for our belief that European folk music is essentially a stylistic unit. Let us also briefly discuss the unity of the continent with regard to individual elements of music—scales, meter, intervals, and manner of singing.

The scales of European folk song exhibit great variety. Most typically, there are songs with only two or three different tones (these are most frequently children's ditties or game songs), there are songs with five tones (pentatonic scales), and others with six or seven tones. But the kinds of intervals, the distances in pitch, among the tones are not quite so diverse. The tendency is for European folk songs to use intervals that fit into the diatonic system, a system of tones that we can find by playing the white keys of the piano. The diatonic system consists of major and minor seconds and of intervals produced by adding seconds. Throughout Europe, it seems that the most common intervals in folk music are the major seconds and the minor thirds. Unfortunately we do not yet have statistics to prove this definitively, but a thorough inspection of a few representative song collections would be convincing. Other intervals are also found, of course, and occasionally there are intervals that do not fit into the diatonic system and which could not even be reproduced approximately on the piano. Also, in folk singing the intervals are not sung with the degree of precision found on the piano, and deviation from a standard norm seems to be somewhat greater in folk than in cultivated music. Nevertheless, adherence to the diatonic intervals seems to be one of the great general characteristics of European folk music. It goes without saying that there are exceptions, and these, indeed, constitute one of the fascinating aspects of our field.

Going into a bit more detail, we find that a great many of the songs that use seven tones can be explained, as far as their tonal material is concerned, in terms of the medieval church modes (Dorian, Phrygian, Lydian, Aeolian, Mixolydian, Locrian, and Ionian) that are used to classify Gregorian chant (in slightly different form) as well as other medieval and Renaissance music. This fact has led some scholars to believe that the styles of European folk music actually originated in the chants of the church. While we must concede the possibility of a great deal of influence of church music on folk song, it seems useful to consider these modes as only a system for classifying folk song. As such, it can be used to classify only those songs which actually have seven tones. For instance, Example 3-3 could be considered a Mixolydian tune.

We might be tempted to classify tunes that have only five tones according to this system of modes, pretending that two tones of the mode are simply absent. The trouble is that we could not prove

EXAMPLE 3-3. Russian folk song in the Mixolydian mode, from Elsa Mahler, *Altrussische Volkslieder aus dem Pečoryland* (Basel: Barenreiter-Verlag, 1951), p. 43.

which tones are lacking. A song with the scale A-C-D-E-G that ends on A could be considered Aeolian or minor—assuming that the missing tones are B and F. But if they were B-flat and F the tune would have to be called Phrygian. And if the lacking tones were B-flat and F-sharp the scale would not fit one of the above-mentioned modes at all. Thus we can hardly accept the blanket statement, made so frequently, that folk music is "modal" in the sense of the Gregorian modes. But a great many European folk songs do fit into the modal system. See Example 3-4 for the various modes that can be fashioned out of a nucleus of five tones in the diatonic system.

EXAMPLE 3-4. Diatonic modes based on a single group of five tones.

Pentatonic songs make up a large proportion of the European body of folk song; their scales are usually composed of major seconds and minor thirds, as in Example 3-5.

Pentatonic songs cannot, however—even with the special kind of

EXAMPLE 3-5. English folk song with a pentatonic scale, from Jan P. Schinhan, ed., *The Music of the Ballads* (Durham, N.C.: Duke University Press, 1957. *The Frank C. Brown Collection of North Carolina Folklore*, vol. 4), p. 184.

pentatonic scale illustrated here—be considered as primarily a European phenomenon. This type of scale is one that Europe shares with a large part of the world, particularly with Northern Asia, with the American Indians, and with Negro Africa. The same is true of the songs with two or three tones, illustrated in Example 3-6.

EXAMPLE 3-6. Tritonic children's ditty, found in various nations with different sets of words.

This restricted kind of scale is found in repertories throughout the world. There are some tribes that have little beyond such a simple configuration of tones in their whole repertory, and most of the world's cultures seem to have at least a few songs with diatonic or tritonic scales. In most cases, these are children's songs, game songs, lullabies, and the songs of simple rituals. It is the widespread distribution of this type of scale, coupled with the simplicity of its songs in other respects, that has led folklorists to assume that in Europe they constitute a remnant of an ancient musical culture. These scholars believe that all music must at some time have been as simple as this, and that the simple songs were driven into a corner of the repertory, as newer, more complex music was invented or brought in under outside influence. Again, in these simple two-tone and three-tone songs, the tendency is for the intervals to be major seconds and minor thirds. In summary then, the seven-tone scales, with their modal arrangements, are a hallmark of European folk music; the pentatonic and the two- and three-tone scales are important in the European tradition and are found in many if not all European folk cultures, but they are equally important elsewhere.

Meter and singing style

Most European folk music adheres to the concept of meter. This means that some regularity of recurrence in the accent pattern of the music is present, though such regularity does not by any means imply the predominance of common or triple meters without deviation. A good deal of European folk music can indeed be classed as isometric; that is, a single metric pattern, such as 4/4, 3/4, 6/8, but also 5/8, 7/8, etc., dominates the song. When several meters are used, these tend to appear in recurring sequences; thus a song, particularly one in Eastern Europe, may have a meter consisting of the regular alternation of 3/8, 4/8, and 5/8 measures (see Example 5-3). But music in which no metric pattern can be detected is not common in European folklore. Deviation from a metric pattern—for example, the elongation of tones at points of rest, near the endings of lines or of phrases—are common, as shown in Example 3-7; but these deviations tend to reinforce the metric character of the music rather than to negate it.

EXAMPLE 3-7. English folk song, "Lady Isabel and the Elf Knight," from Cecil Sharp, *English Folk Songs from the Southern Appalachians* (London, New York: Oxford University Press, 1952), vol. 1, p. 7.

Thus another trait, found also, to be sure, elsewhere in the world, ties European folk music into a homogeneous unit.

The manner of singing—use of the voice, movements and facial expressions, types of tone color—is another important feature. We have few guidelines according to which we can describe this phenomenon. Alan Lomax[2] is one of the few scholars who have paid attention to this important aspect of music. Lomax believes that it is possible to divide the world into relatively few areas each of which has a particular manner of singing that exists independent of the geographic distribution of other aspects of musical style such as melody, rhythm, and form. Europe, he finds, is rather complicated, for it possesses a number of singing styles that do not have contiguous distribution.

[2] Alan Lomax, "Folk Song Style," *American Anthropologist* LXI (1959), 927-54.

The three singing styles that Lomax assigns to European folk music are termed by him as "Old European," "Modern European," and "Eurasian." The "Eurasian" style, which is found primarily throughout most of the high cultures of Asia, is represented in Europe in parts of the British Isles and France, in South Italy, and in the Mohammedan parts of the Balkans. The singing is high-pitched, strident, and harsh, and the singers' facial expressions are rigidly controlled or sad. The style lends itself well to long, ornamented tones and passages, and the character of the music is sweetly sad and melancholy. Lomax equates singing styles with certain types of social structure and, according to him, the Eurasian area is one in which the position of women is below that of men; they may be put on a pedestal, but they do not have equality.

The "Old European" style of Lomax is found in the Hebrides, Northern England, Scandinavia, the Pyrenees, Czechoslovakia, Western Yugoslavia, Northern Italy, Germany, parts of the Balkans, the Ukraine, and the Caucasus. Here the singing is done with the throat relaxed, and the facial expressions of the singers are lively and animated. The tunes are simple and unornamented, and group singing is common. Cooperation among the singers in a chorus seems to have allowed polyphony to develop, and, says Lomax, possibly some of the polyphonic types of folk music have antedated the development of polyphony in European cultivated music. In these areas, in any event, harmony was easily accepted. The idea of cooperation in music seems to have something to do with social cooperation, for the position of women in the "Old European" areas, according to Lomax, has been one of equality with men.

The "Modern European" style is, according to Lomax, a later layer which seems to have been superimposed on some of the other styles, perhaps because of the influence of the cities. It is found in most of England and France, in Hungary, Central Italy, and colonial America. This is the area of ballads and lyrical love songs. Singing, in contrast to the Old European style, is normally done by soloists or in unblended unison. The vocal quality is harsh and strained. Interest is more in the words than in the music.

Lomax's observations are certainly stimulating. He believes that the way in which people sing is more likely to remain constant than is the musical content of their songs. And he believes that a small sample of singing from a particular area or country will indicate the

Spain
Tris-tes nue-vas ij
Rumänia Adagio
Foa - ie vor - de trei a - lu -
England (Sussex)
As I rode ov - er Salis - bur - y plain, twas
se can - ta - ban en Se - vi - lla
ne, ci - ne n'a - re scâr băn lu - me,
there I met a young scamp - ing blade;
se ha ca sa - do el Con-de Al - ba con da -
vi - e săi dau de la - mi - ne,
he kiss - ed me and en - tic - ed me

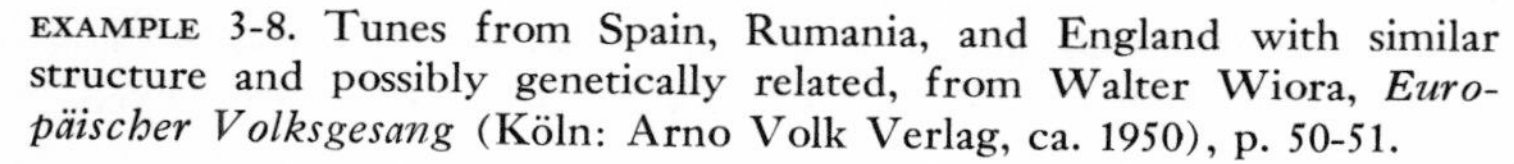

EXAMPLE 3-8. Tunes from Spain, Rumania, and England with similar structure and possibly genetically related, from Walter Wiora, *Europäischer Volksgesang* (Köln: Arno Volk Verlag, ca. 1950), p. 50-51.

total singing style of that area. He seems to feel, accordingly, that each culture can sing in only one way (which is a theory that has been proved incorrect in various cultures, as for instance among the North American Indians). But Lomax's observations do lead us to conclude that Europe is not a unit as far as singing style is concerned, but that two or three styles of singing and voice production are found, and that each of these is supranational in character and cuts across the boundaries of politics, culture, and language. Also he shows that the two main European singing styles are not found to a great extent on other continents (except among descendants of Europeans).

Wandering melodies

Quite aside from the characteristics of the elements of music, the content of the tunes found in Europe indicates that Europe is a historical unit. In the nineteenth century, some scholars began to be intrigued by what they came to call "wandering melodies," that is, by tunes whose variants were found in the folk traditions of widely separated countries. The existence of such tunes is generally recognized. Example 3-8 illustrates this phenomenon, but great numbers of related tunes found in a larger number of countries can be seen in several publications, particularly in Wiora's *Europäischer Volksgesang*.[3] In a good many cases it is quite likely that the similar

[3] Wiora, *Europäischer Volksgesang*, p. 5f.

tunes found in several nations are indeed wandering melodies or, rather, variants of a single wandering melody. Whether or not the three tunes in Example 3-8 are genetically related we cannot say. Curiously, the variants of a tune found in separated countries are usually accompanied by widely varying verbal texts. An English ballad tune that has related forms in other countries will hardly be found outside England with a translation of the same ballad story. This very fact may lead us to suspect that the existence of similar tunes in different countries is not always—and perhaps not even frequently—simply the result of a tune's migration. In any event, we cannot *prove* in most cases that the tune has actually migrated. It is likely that traveling singers of the early Middle Ages (their existence is documented) taught to the peoples of many lands the original forms of many songs which developed into groups of melodies related in the manner of Example 3-8.

Another way of explaining the phenomenon of "wandering melodies" is that the musical characteristics of European folk song have been so homogeneous and have developed so much in the same direction throughout the continent that similar tunes were composed independently in several countries. Given a certain restricted set of musical characteristics—for the sake of argument, let's assume melodies composed of five tones with seconds and thirds predominating, regular metric structure, the tendency for the final sections of songs and of phrases to be lower in pitch and more drawn-out rhythmically than the rest, and a range of about an octave—it might be possible and even necessary for similar tunes to spring up independently in several places at various times. Thus the fact that there are some obvious similarities among the tunes in the foregoing Examples does not prove that all of them are descended, through the use of communal re-creation, from a single parent tune. But whichever explanation is the correct one (and we may never know in many specific cases), the existence of similar tunes throughout the continent again shows us that Europe is an entity as far as its folk music is concerned.

Some song types found in Europe

Europe is a unit not only in the purely musical aspects of folk song. The cultural background and context as well as the words of the songs also indicate the essential integrity of the continent. There are certain types of songs that are found throughout Europe, though they are not present everywhere in the same proportion of quantity and importance. Take the area of narrative song, for example. In Europe there are two main types of songs that tell stories, the ballad and the epic. Narrative songs are found here and there in the traditional music of other continents, but they are not common. In Europe, on the other hand, they occupy a position of preëminence, although they are more important in some countries than in others.

The ballad was developed in Europe in the Middle Ages—first, presumably, by song composers of city and court—and evidently passed into oral tradition and the repertories of folk cultures thereafter. The musical characteristics of the ballad are not different from those of most other kinds of folk song. Usually there are three to six musical lines and a number of stanzas. As far as the words are concerned, the ballad tells a story involving one main event. In contrast to the ballads, the epic songs are long, complex, and involve several events tied together by a common theme. Typically, the epic, as exemplified perhaps by the "guslar" epics of the Southern Slavs, does not have a strophic arrangement but tends rather to use a line which, with variations, is repeated many times. But there are sub-types of these genres and it is at times difficult to distinguish between them. (See Chapter 4 for more detail about ballads, Chapter 6 for epics.)

Love songs are important in many European countries, and they are relatively rare in the folklore of other continents. They are more common in Western Europe than in the East, and characteristically they express their feelings of love for another person in a melancholy or tragic setting. Again, the music of love songs does not, on the whole, differ in style from that of other folk songs.

A number of ceremonial song types are common throughout Europe. Of course, the use of folk songs in an ecclesiastical setting is found. There are areas in which genuine folk hymns are sung; in Germany, a body of spiritual folk song became a partial basis of the Lutheran hymn, and the singing of "Kyrieleis" (a corruption of "Kyrie Eleison") in the rural communities was reported in medieval sources. But more typical are songs involving ceremonies that may have been practiced long before the advent of Christianity in Europe. Thus there are songs which revolve around important events or turning points in a person's life: puberty, birth, marriage, and death. In some countries these proliferated, as in France, where special songs for various events in a child's life (first words, first walking, etc.) were developed. The French have songs to urge a child to eat, to teach him to count, and so on. These are songs accompanying the so-called rites of passage which are important in practically every culture.

Also, there are songs involving the turning points in the year, such as the advent of spring, the summer and winter solstices, and the equinox. These have frequently been associated also with agriculture, and some have been attached, since the introduction of Christianity, to Christian festivals. Thus, some pre-Christian winter solstice songs have become Christmas songs—as may have been the case of the popular German "O Tannenbaum." Pagan spring songs have sometimes become Easter or Whitsuntide songs. Again, these calendric song types are common in several nations of Europe.

Songs involving agriculture are also common, but more so in Eastern than in Western Europe. Perhaps these songs should be generally regarded as work songs, since some of them actually aid in the rhythm of work, while others, such as the short tunes used by the Lapps to call reindeer, are functional in labor but not in a rhythmic sense. Another type of agricultural song, simply describing the work, is not sung during work, however, but perhaps at social gatherings in the evening. Again, work songs are found also in other continents, but they are more common in Europe than in most other areas; and, as before, we cannot say that their style differs appreciably from the styles of European folk songs at large. Of course, a few types of work songs do have special musical styles. Thus the Tribbiera of Corsica (Example 3-9), a type of work song sung while driving oxen around a small enclosure in which threshing is done, always has a form consisting of two sections with words followed by a long, melismatic call.

Dance music is of course one of the main types of folk and ethnic music throughout the world. In Europe it is one of the important genres, and accompanies two main types of dance. According to Herzog,[4] the older dances are involved with rituals and ceremonies (round dances are especially characteristic here); these tend to be accompanied by relatively simple music. Dances that came into the

[4] George Herzog, "Song," Funk and Wagnalls' *Standard Dictionary of Folklore, Mythology, and Legend* (New York, 1949-50), II, 1035.

European folk repertory at later times—and this includes most of those danced by couples, and many of the other kinds of social dances—have more complex music which shows, as does the dance itself, the influence of sophisticated musical cultures. However, while we can in good conscience make such broad generalizations

EXAMPLE 3-9. Corsican "Tribbiera," from Wolfgang Laade, "The Corsican Tribbiera, a kind of work song," *Ethnomusicology* 6 (1962), 185.

about folk dance and dance music, we must also stress the tremendous variety of dances which exists in Europe. The dance seems to be one area of culture in which European trends are similar or closely related to those in other continents. Possibly this means that the older layers of European culture, those which antedate the introduction of Christianity, and which stem from a time when the European folk cultures would have been classed as primitive or nonliterate, have remained present in the dance more than in some other aspects of culture.

At any rate, mimetic dances (those which choreographically represent actions, events, feelings, persons, or animals) are found throughout European folk culture and in other continents as well. The same is true of dances with weapons (sword dances, for instance, are performed in Scotland, Central Europe, and India), dances having sexual symbolism, and acrobatic dances, to name just a few. Gertrude Kurath[5] has made a survey of European folk dances and has managed to divide the vast array into several types, according to the form and style of dancing. For example, she distinguishes among

[5] Gertrude P. Kurath, "Dance," Funk and Wagnalls' *Standard Dictionary of Folklore, Mythology, and Legend* (New York, 1949-50), I, 276-96.

circle, longway (line), and quadrille (square) dances, according to the formation used by the dancers. The point is, again, that each of these forms is found all over Europe, and that similar dances are performed in areas and countries that have sharply contrasting cultures. Thus, Kurath cites the Maypole as being present in dances in Spain, England, Germany, and Hungary; the "Hey," a technique in which two lines of dancers wind in and out of a circle, is found in England, Germany, Czechoslovakia, and Spain. Thus—in spite of national and regional peculiarities—we see again the basic unity of European folklore.

Another characteristic type in European folk music is the humorous song. Musically this type does not differ especially from other songs, and of course humorous words can be associated with all sorts of song functions—ballads, work songs, children's songs, and so forth. One special type of humorous song found in many countries is the cumulative song. It is not always uproariously funny or even mildly amusing, although some elements of humor are usually found and perhaps even the process of cumulation can be considered as having a humorous effect. A cumulative song is one in which each stanza, while presenting something new, also incorporates elements from the previous stanzas. Among the best known of these songs are "The Twelve Days of Christmas" and, of course, "Alouette."

Instruments and instrumental music

Musical instruments are important in the European folk music tradition, but it is a fact that singing accounts for the preponderance of music making, formal and informal. Still, the instrumental music is of tremendous interest. While we can state with confidence that the participation of the population in singing is quite general, that is, most people in a folk culture can sing some songs and recognize many more, instruments are to a much larger extent the property of specialists. As we have pointed out, truly professional musicians are rarely found in folk cultures. There are not many who really can play an instrument to the satisfaction of a whole village, and only a few persons can make instruments. Moreover, instrumental music is much more commonly used simply as entertainment than are songs.

According to Curt Sachs[6] and others, the primitive instrumental styles of the world did not come about through simple imitation, on instruments, of the vocal melodies. To be sure, vocal music must have come into existence before instrumental. But instrumental music presumably came about through the elevation of noise-making gadgets to really musical artifacts, through the coincidences of acoustic phenomena accidentally discovered, and through visual criteria used by craftsmen. For example, the scales on flutes may be constructed not only with particular intervals in mind, but also with the visual effect of the spacing of the finger holes. If this assumption is correct, it should not be surprising that the instrumental music of European folk cultures often seems quite unrelated to the songs found in the same area and sung by the same people. Also, there seems to be more stylistic variety in the instrumental music of Europe than in the vocal music, perhaps because of the limitations of human voice and ear as compared with the relative freedom allowed the instrumentalist, who needs to know only the right motions to make, but not necessarily how the music will sound before he plays it. Random improvisation and toying with the instrument may have a considerable effect on developing the styles of instrumental folk music.

Regarding the instruments themselves, we can make few generalizations about Europe. On the one hand, European folk instruments—especially the simpler ones—have much in common with some of the instruments of nonliterate cultures. Some—recorder-like plugged flutes, for example—are found on all continents. Instruments once thought to be as characteristically European as bagpipes are also found throughout Asia. On the other hand, the folk cultures of Europe have frequently taken over instruments from urban civilization. Thus some of the typical folk music instruments of Eastern Europe today are the ordinary violin (perhaps slightly modified) and the clarinet, in simpler forms. More interestingly, some of the older instruments from the cities such as the psaltery or dulcimer and the autoharp are still in use in folk culture.

In Chapters 4-6 we shall explore European folk music in somewhat more detail. Unfortunately, even if comprehensive information were available we could not give the whole story on these pages. We

[6] Curt Sachs, *The Wellsprings of Music* (The Hague, Martinus Nijhoff, 1962), p. 110f.

cannot even give samples of the music of each nation. All we can do is to give some examples of what is typical, what is common, and what is particularly noteworthy, and then to hope that the reader will continue delving into the specialized literature and, above all, proceed with listening in order to broaden his understanding of this fascinating area of European culture.

Bibliography

The only general and comprehensive book on European folk music is in German, and it approaches its field from a very special viewpoint, attempting to show various historical layers evident in present-day traditions. Nevertheless, it is worth reading: Werner Danckert, *Das europäische Volkslied* (Berlin: B. Hahnefeld, 1939). Several collections of folk music in Europe that make it possible to compare the various styles are Leonhard Deutsch, *A Treasury of the World's Finest Folk Song* (New York: Howell, Siskin, 1942); Maud Karpeles, *Folk Song of Europe* (London: Novello, 1956); *Europäische Lieder in den Ursprachen* (Berlin: Merseburger, 1956), a collection published under the auspices of UNESCO; and Walter Wiora, *Europäischer Volksgesang* (Cologne: Arno Volk, 1955), a collection that stresses the unity of European folk song by presenting variants of the same tunes from several countries.

Introductions to the field of European balladry are Gordon H. Gerould, *The Ballad of Tradition* (Oxford: Clarendon Press, 1932) and William J. Entwistle, *European Balladry* (Oxford: Clarendon Press, 1939). The many variants of a single ballad text in several European nations are studied in Iivar Kemppinen, *The Ballad of Lady Isabel and the False Knight* (Helsinki: Published by the author, 1954). A short discussion of European epics is Felix Hoerburger's "Correspondence Between Eastern and Western Folk Epics," *J-IFMC,* IV (1952), 23-26. The entire epic tradition is discussed, but with emphasis on the Yugoslav forms, in Albert B. Lord, *The Singer of Tales* (Cambridge: Harvard University Press, 1960). Finally, a classic on folk song as a living artifact is Phillips Barry, "The Transmission of Folk Song," *Journal of American Folklore,* XXVII (1914), 67-76.

4

The Germanic Peoples

The Germanic peoples—that is, those peoples which speak Germanic languages—can be divided into three groups on the basis of their folklore: 1) the English, including Scotland and Ireland; 2) the Scandinavians; and 3) the Dutch and the German-speaking peoples of Germany, Austria, most of Switzerland, and other areas in Eastern Europe. Although these three groups of peoples speak related languages, their cultures cannot be considered particularly similar, and this is also true of the styles of their folk music. Of course, the folk music of the Germanic peoples is known in different phases and varying degrees. For the English-speaking peoples there exists a vast body of ballads, collected in England as well as in America; and the study of ballad variants, their interrelationship, structure, and origin, has been carried further for English material than elsewhere. Of German folklore we know best the songs that have come into the repertory rather recently. Swedish folk music happens to have available a large collection of fiddle tunes, because some Swedish collectors have concentrated on this aspect of music. Also, the Germanic peoples have been strongly influenced by their neighbors. For example, English folk song shows considerable relationship to that of the Low Countries and France, while German folk music is at times similar to that of its neighbors to the east, Czechoslovakia, Poland, and Hungary, and Austrian folk songs have some common features with those of Italy. Thus, while we are treating the Germanic peoples as a unit in one chapter, it should not be assumed that their folk music is necessarily a stylistic unit. We should avoid the corresponding conclusion that the style of Germanic musics goes back to the time when all Germanic peoples were one and spoke one tongue, and the equally erroneous assumption that the Germanic-speaking peoples possess a psychic unity. The heritage of Germanic languages goes back much further than the style of present-day folk music, and whatever similarities are found are due almost certainly to cultural contact in recent times, that is, from the early Middle Ages on.

The English Child ballads

The most characteristic type of British folk song is the ballad, and the most famous ballads are the Child ballads. These have nothing to do with children but rather bear the name of Francis James Child (1825-96), who organized, published, and classified those ballads which he assumed were of popular (that is, rural and truly anonymous) origin. He avoided, in his classification, those ballads in the folk tradition which could be traced to the cities or to professional song writers, and those which he thought did not have high literary quality. Because the different variants of each ballad do not bear identical titles or first lines, he gave each ballad (or group of variants) a number, and for this reason the most famous ballads are known by their "Child numbers."

The most famous of the English ballads should be known to the reader: Child 2, "The Elfin Knight"; Child 10, "The Two Sisters";

Child 12, "Lord Randall"; Child 13, "Edward"; Child 53, "Lord Bateman" or "Young Beichan"; Child 54, "The Cherry Tree Carol"; Child 73, "Lord Thomas and Fair Elinor" (or fair Annet); Child 75, "Lord Lovel"; Child 81, "Little Musgrave and Lady Barnard" or "Little Mathy Grove"; Child 84, "Barbara Allen"; Child 95, "The Maid Freed from the Gallows"; Child 155, "Sir Hugh" or "The Jew's Daughter"; Child 173, "Lady Hamilton"; Child 200, "The Gypsy Laddie"; Child 243, "James Harris" or "The Daemon Lover" or "The House Carpenter"; Child 277, "The Wife Wrapped in Wether's Skin"; and Child 286, "The Golden Vanity" or "The Sweet Trinity."

There are about three hundred Child ballads, but for only about two hundred has any music been collected; for the rest, only words survive. The famous ballads we have enumerated share some characteristics, and they are representative of the whole Child group (with the exception of a number dealing with Robin Hood), although most of the ones mentioned here are tragic, while the majority of the whole group of Child ballads actually do not have unhappy endings. The stories of these ballads are easily available in most of the large array of folk song collections made in the United States, and in Child's own collection, which dates from the late nineteenth century.[1] The story usually revolves around one incident, names of places and characters change from variant to variant, and setting and background are only briefly stated. The narrator does not take an active part in the story but tells it dispassionately. There is some dialogue, and there is also a tendency for whole verses to be virtually repeated, as in the following excerpt from Child 200:[2]

(*He says*): *Take off, take off those milk-white gloves,*
Those shoes of Spanish leather,
And hand you down your lily-white hand,
We'll bid farewell together.

(*Narrator says*): *Oh she took off those milk-white gloves,*
Those shoes of Spanish leather,
And she handed him down her lily-white hand,
They bade farewell forever.

[1] Francis James Child, *The English and Scottish Popular Ballads*, 5 vols. (Boston and New York: Houghton, Mifflin, and Co., 1882-98); reprinted, New York: Folklore Associates, 1956.

[2] Cecil J. Sharp, *English Folk Songs from the Southern Appalachians* (London: Oxford University Press, 1952), I, 235.

Other characteristics of ballads are also found in this example. We see the use of conceits, that is, of descriptive phrases which appear repeatedly as if they were formulae. Thus, hands are often described as "lily-white" (as are gloves), horses are "milk-white," and so on. Many ballads have refrains, the origins of which are sometimes obscure. Flowers, plants, and spices are sometimes mentioned, as in Child 1:[3]

(*Verse*) *Go tell her to make me a cambric shirt*
(*Refrain*) *Setherwood, sale, rosemary and thyme,*
(*Verse*) *Without any needle or needle's work,*
And then she'll be a true lover of mine.

Refrains, incidentally, are a feature of song that is shared by all regions of Europe. Some refrains mention dancing or movements that can be interpreted as parts of a dance. Here is an excerpt from "The Two Sisters" (Child 10):[4]

There lived an old lord in the North countree
(*Refrain*) *Bow down, bow down.*
There lived an old lord in the north countree
(*Refrain*) *Very true to you. . . .*

"Bow down" is thought to be related to dancing. The reason for mentioning this is a theory that the ballad, narrative though it is, began as a dance song type. The name may, of course, be derived from the Latin *ballare* (to dance), and there is some evidence that ballads were once used as dance songs in medieval Scandinavia. On the Faeroe Islands, between Scotland and Norway, this tradition is still in existence, and lively group dances using the "Faeroe step" (two steps left, one right) may be performed while the dancers sing Norwegian ballads. We know of no ballad dancing in the English-speaking world, but this practice may once have existed there as well.

A look at the collections of Child or of some of the more recent great American collectors makes it obvious that the differences among variants of one ballad can be tremendous. Take Child 12, the popular "Lord Randall." Randall's name appears in all sorts of variant forms, Randall, Rendal, Lorendo, Durango, William, Tyranty, Nelson, Elson, King Henery, Willie Doo, etc. The person who poisons him may be his sweetheart, his grandmother, or his step-

[3] Sharp, *English Folk Songs*, I, 1.
[4] Sharp, *English Folk Songs*, I, 27.

mother. It has even been established that the children's song, "Oh where have you been, Billy boy, Billy boy?" which ends, "She's a young thing and cannot leave her mother" was derived from the more dramatic "Lord Randall," or something like it. Thus it would seem that formulae are very stable elements, while the details of a story are more subject to change. The lengths of the variants also differ greatly. A story told in one ballad with the use of fourteen stanzas may be, in another version, summarized in four, through elision, omission of events, and omission of stanzas giving background information.

Similar variety is found in the tunes. Bertrand H. Bronson[5] has assembled all of the tunes used for the Child ballads, and he finds that for each ballad story there seem to be two or three basic tunes to which all of the variants must be sung. For example, most of the tunes of "The Golden Vanity" (Child 286) are related to one of the two in Examples 4-1 and 4-2.

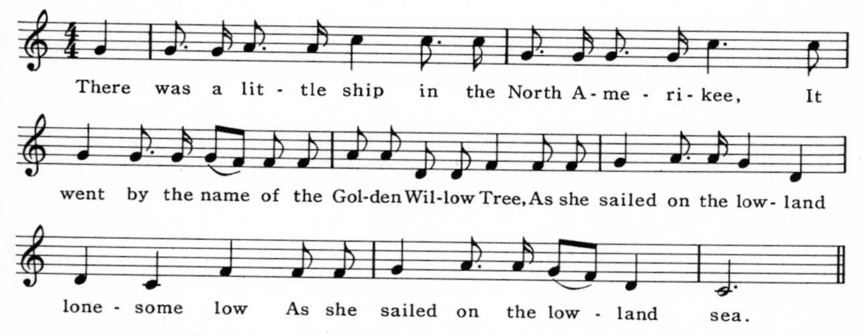

EXAMPLE 4-1. English folk song, "The Sweet Trinity," from Jan P. Schinhan, ed., *The Music of the Ballads* (Durham, N.C.: Duke University Press, 1957. *The Frank C. Brown Collection of North Carolina Folklore*, vol. 4), p. 120.

While ballad stories evidently moved from nation to nation in the Middle Ages, the tunes did not accompany them. For example, there is the ballad of "Lady Isabel and the Elf-Knight" (Child 2), in which a knight courts a lady but really intends to kill and rob her; when she discovers his false intentions, she foils him and causes him to drown. This ballad is known throughout Europe except for the

[5] Bertrand Harris Bronson, *The Traditional Tunes of the Child Ballads* (Princeton, N.J.: Princeton University Press, 1958–).

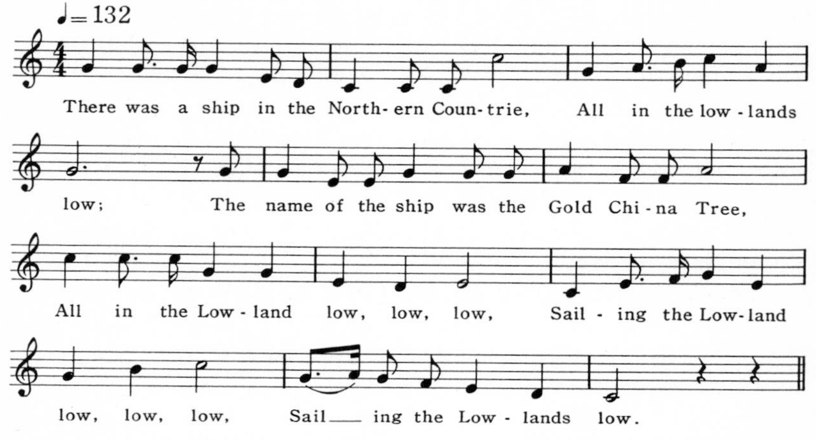

EXAMPLE 4-2. English folk song, "The Little Cabin Boy," from Phillips Barry, Fannie H. Eckstrom and Mary W. Smyth, *British Ballads from Maine* (New Haven, Conn.: Yale University Press, 1929), p. xxxiii.

Balkan area, but its tunes are largely national in provenience, and the tunes used with the English versions are evidently not related to those used in Dutch, Scandinavian, German, or other versions. On the other hand, a tune used for one ballad in the English repertory may be found in other English ballads or songs.

Broadside ballads

Besides the Child ballads, for which no written original can usually be found, the English-language repertory possesses other types, particularly a group of later origin, the broadside ballads. This type, so named because it appeared printed on large sheets of paper called broadsides, became popular throughout Western Europe. Written frequently by professional song writers, the broadside ballads tend to deal with historical events more than do the popular ballads, and they contrast with the Child ballads also in their concern for detail, in their more complex plots, and in the involvement of the narrator, who frequently appends a moral. The words are often shamelessly sentimental and usually do not have the literary value of the older ballads. But the broadside ballads (which were still being written in the twentieth century) functioned somewhat as newspapers in areas in which illiteracy was common. All of them did not, of course, pass into oral tradition, but a good many of them did and have thus become true folk songs. Some of our best-known songs originated as English broadside ballads: "The Foggy Dew," made popular by Carl Sandburg, "Brennan on the Moor," "Devilish Mary," and "Sam Hall." Some of the broadsides are even derived from the Child ballads. Thus, a broadside ballad called "The Turkish Lady" appeared, but it is obviously just a variant of "Lord Bateman" (Child 53), in which a Turkish lady saves an English prisoner in her father's jail and marries him. The tunes of the broadside ballads are of diverse origin. Many of the printed broadsides did not include music but simply stated that the song was to be sung to the tune of this or that popular song, folk song, or hymn. Thus many of these ballads are sung to tunes belonging to music hall songs, hymns, and older ballads. Finally, the practice of printing broadside ballads and their dissemination into folk tradition is found not only in Britain but also in most European countries and, of course, in America.

The style of English folk music

As we have pointed out, the music of the English ballads does not differ greatly from that of English folk song in general; thus, the discussion of ballad tunes below can be said to apply to English folk song at large. Many of the older tunes have, as one characteristic, a melodic contour which forms, roughly, an arc, starting low, rising in the second phrase, remaining on the higher level of tessitura in the third phrase, and moving down to the level of the first in the fourth phrase. Four phrases or lines are common, but of course five (usually through repetition of the fourth), six, and eight are also found, as well as two and three. Three examples of English folk song follow (Examples 4-3, 4-4, and 4-5); they may be considered representative of the whole style to an extent, but we should remember that certain song types, such as dance songs, game ditties, children's songs, and humorous songs are not represented. Example 4-3 is a Scots version of Child 76, as sung by Ewan MacColl, the well-known folk singer. Example 4-4 is a variant of the same song collected in Southern Indiana. It is essentially the same melody, but is sung in quite a different manner. Example 4-5 is the tune of a broadside ballad, "Girls of Newfoundland," of Irish origin, collected in Labrador. Perhaps we should point out here that much more British folk music has been collected in North America than in Britain, and that, for material collected in England itself, published collections with reliable transcriptions are difficult to come by. Thus we must rely to some extent on American versions for a picture of British folk music.

EXAMPLE 4-3. English folk song, "Lord Gregory." Reprinted from *The Traditional Tunes of the Child Ballads*, vol. 2 by Bertrand Harris Brown by permission of Princeton University Press, Copyright 1962.

EXAMPLE 4-4. English folk song, "The Lass of Loch Royal," from Bruno Nettl, "The Musical Style of English Ballads Collected in Indiana," *Acta Musicologica* 27 (1955), 83.

Examples 4-3 and 4-4 use the so-called "ballad meter," that is, iambic lines alternating in three- and four-foot lengths (- / - / - / - /; - / - / - /; and so forth). This is common—though by no means universal—in British folk song and tends, in music, to be translated into one of two types of rhythm: $\frac{4}{4}$ ♩ | ♩ ♩ ♩ ♩ | ♩ ♩ ♩ or ♩ | ♩ ♩ ♩. ♩ | ♩ ♩ ♩. Example 4-3 uses the first of these, and Example 4-4, a variant of the second. There is frequently an elongation or a shortening of measures, or even heterometric structure; thus, in Example 4-4 the meas-

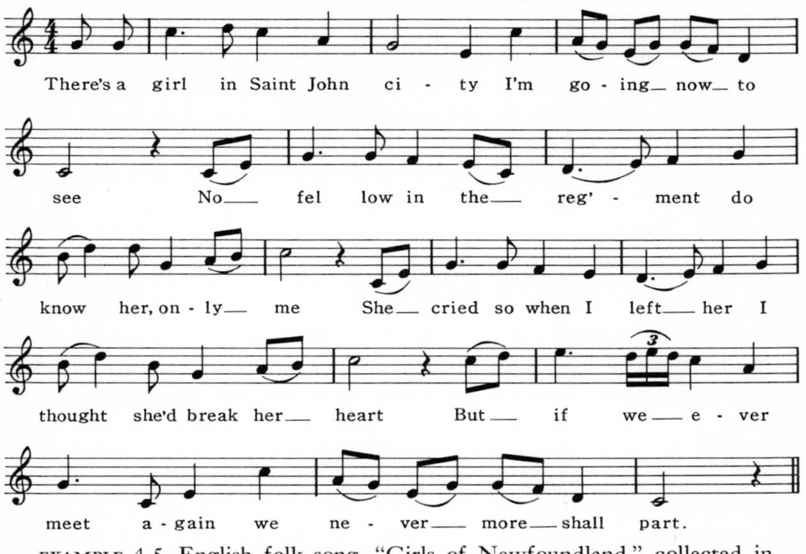

EXAMPLE 4-5. English folk song, "Girls of Newfoundland," collected in Newfoundland by MacEdward Leach, transcribed by Bruno Nettl.

ures have, respectively, 5, 5, 6, 5, 7, 6, 6, and 8 eighths. Example 4-5 also has similar structure to Example 4-3, but the length of the text is doubled over that in Example 4-4, so there are four lines of four feet, and four of three feet. When this kind of stanza occurs, it is usually translated, musically, into four long lines whose rhythm is almost always a variant of ♩ | ♩ ♩ ♩ ♩ | ♩ ♩ ♩ ♩ | ♩ ♩ ♩ ♩ | 𝅗𝅥 or ♪ | ♩ ♪♩ ♪ | ♩ ♪♩ ♪ | ♩ ♪♩ ♪ | ♩. ♩ . This longer kind of form is more common in the broadside ballads than in the older songs such as the Child ballads.

British folk song is frequently said to be modal, but the great majority of the songs fall into the major or Ionian mode. There are also a good many in the Mixolydian (major with lowered seventh) mode, in Dorian (minor with raised sixth), and in Aeolian (natural minor). The other modes are not common. Our three examples, however, are all major. Some modulation may occur (though this is often hard to identify because the music is monophonic) as in Example 4-3, in which the first two phrases seem to have G for a tonic, but the last one, D.

Much has also been said of the pentatonic nature of English folk song. Actually, relatively few of the songs are strictly pentatonic, while the majority (again, except for the old layer of children's and related songs) seems to be heptatonic or hexatonic. It is sometimes useful to examine the functions of the various tones in a scale, however, for often it will be evident that the most important and most common tones are indeed five in number, while the other two are subsidiary or used only in ornaments. Also, the scale structure of the individual phrases or lines may be pentatonic. For instance, in Example 4-3, the first half of the song uses a common kind of pentatonic scale—D, F-sharp, G, A, B; the other tones, E and C-sharp, are brought in only later. This kind of thing is also found in Example 4-4, in which the important tones are B, C (tonic), E, F, and G. Example 4-6, a version of Child 53, uses six tones, but one of them, F, appears only in ornaments. This song also is a good example of the kind of pentatonism found in English folk music.

EXAMPLE 4-6. English folk song, "Lord Bateman," from Bruno Nettl, "The Musical Style of English Ballads Collected in Indiana," *Acta Musicologica* 27 (1955), 83.

Béla Bartók[6] has divided Hungarian folk singing into two types, which he called "parlando-rubato" (mentioned in Chapter 1) and "tempo-giusto." The distinction between these two ways of singing does not always emerge from printed music, since it involves the singer's interpretation of rhythm and tempo. Parlando-rubato singing emphasizes the words, frequently uses elaborate ornamentation

[6] Béla Bartók, *Hungarian Folk Music* (London: Oxford University Press, 1931).

such as trills and glides (Example 4-4), puts heavy stress on certain tones and considerable tension on the vocal cords, and tends to deviate from the established rhythmic and metric patterns through the use of rubato. Tempo-giusto singing sticks more closely to meter and tempo and has less ornamentation. Although this distinction was derived for use in describing Hungarian folk music, it applies also to singing in other countries, especially those of Northern and Eastern Europe. Example 4-3 is a sample of tempo giusto singing, while Example 4-4, a variant of the same song, exemplifies the parlando-rubato. Both styles are found in the British ballad tradition. In Hungarian folk music, parlando-rubato is used mainly for ballads and tempo-giusto for dance songs.

The emphasis on pentatonic structure does not seem to be an ingredient of the newer layer of British song. The tunes that were introduced into the folk culture more recently, perhaps since the advent of music printing and the broadside ballad in the sixteenth century, are both more varied in style and more closely related to popular and art music. This is to be expected, of course, with regard to the broadsides, since their writers frequently set them to tunes of any sort that were widely current. Thus the later tunes are more frequently in major or harmonic minor, rarely pentatonic, and they do not deviate—as does Example 4-4—from a standard and consistent metric structure.

At this point we must mention also the Celtic-speaking inhabitants of the British Isles, particularly the Irish and the Welsh, peoples whose musical culture has played so important a part in their history that the Irish national emblem is the harp. Irish folk song today is almost entirely in the English language, and, indeed, the songs of Irish origin have contributed greatly to the English-language heritage of the United States, Canada, and Australia. On the whole, their musical style does not differ greatly from that of the English folk tunes of eighteenth- and nineteenth-century origin.

The Welsh have developed—partly through their folk heritage and partly because of the influence of hymn singing—a tradition of choral singing of folk songs; this is done largely in the style of nineteenth-century hymns, with conventional chord progressions and triadic harmony. The Welsh have, in modern folklore, preserved an instrument that evidently was widespread in medieval art music, the *crwth* or *crowd*, a lyre with six strings—four over the fingerboard, two as drones—which was usually bowed. It evidently accompanied the songs of the bards, whose importance among the Welsh and Irish was very great, much as a similar instrument, the *tallharpa*, was used in Finland and Estonia.

Some Netherlandish folk dances

Of course, the ballads are not the only kinds of folk songs in the British Isles; we have chosen them as one representative group. The same sort of thing is true of the Dutch and Flemish folk dances, which are briefly discussed here because we can discuss only one of the categories of Dutch music, and because we need to pay some attention to the dance music of the Germanic-speaking nations.

Evidently folk dancing has indeed been a prominent activity in the Low Countries for centuries. An edict of Charlemagne outlawed dancing in churches and ceremonies, indicating the popularity of such activities. The practice of religious dance, including dances on the occasion of death, particularly of young girls, is attested by various documents from history, and appears to have remained in the folk tradition until relatively recent times. The religious dances are almost always round dances.

In other ways, also, Dutch folk music seems to have had a close relationship to the practices of Christian worship. There are many religious folk songs and carols of various kinds (Christmas and Easter), and the style of a great deal of Dutch folk music reminds us of the styles of the Christian monophonic hymns and the Lutheran chorales. To a considerable degree this is true of German folk music, as well, for it in many instances also adheres to the style of the hymn, with its typical lines consisting mainly of quarter notes except for the final long tone.

Many European folk dances have their origin in pre-Christian ritual dancing. An example from Holland is the "Seven Sault" dance, described by Kunst,[7] and known also in other parts of Western Europe. It was evidently once a sacrificial dance, but after the introduction of Christianity it was danced at harvest festivals, fairs, and wedding parties. These functions are, of course, residual of pre-

[7] Jaap Kunst, "On Dutch Folk Dances and Dance Tunes," *Studies in Ethnomusicology* I (1961), 35.

Christian ceremonies involving the life cycle or the changes in the year's cycle. Kunst reports seeing the Seven Saults still performed in the twentieth century on the Dutch island of Terschelling. It involves seven motions of a mildly acrobatic nature: stamping with each foot, touching the ground with each knee, then with each elbow, and finally with the nose. It was evidently performed—as are many European folk dances—with the accompaniment of group singing, such as that found in Example 4-7.

EXAMPLE 4-7. Dutch folk dance tune, from Jaap Kunst, "On Dutch Folk Dances and Dance Tunes" in *Studies in Ethnomusicology*, ed. M. Kolinski (New York: Oak Publications, 1961), vol. 1, p. 32.

The tune in Example 4-7 shows us some of the traits common in Western European folk dance music. Of course, since the music is used for dancing, and since it is sung by a group, it could not easily partake of the parlando-rubato singing style with its distortion of tempo and emphasis on words. It tends to be rigid in this aspect of music, to have simple rhythms consisting largely of two- or three-note values (as in this case, quarter, eighth, and sixteenth notes). This tune also is in major, with an implication of harmony in the Western tradition, based on tonic, subdominant, dominant, and dominant seventh chords.

Holland, being near the center of the Germanic-speaking area, exhibits musical relationships to England, Germany, and Scandinavia. In the field of dance and dance music, a number of similarities between Dutch and Scandinavian folk music are striking. Variants of the same tunes and dance movements are found in both areas, as well as in Scotland, which was at one time under strong Danish and Norse influence.

Samples of Scandinavian folk music

The folk music of Scandinavia is of great interest because in some ways it seems to exhibit very ancient traits, and in other ways it has been very much under the influence of the cultivated tradition of the cities. An example of ancient practice frequently cited is the use of parallel fifths in Iceland, which has evidently preserved some medieval traits of Norwegian culture. For a long time there raged an argument—mentioned in Chapter 3—about the origin of Icelandic "organum," whether it represents a case of medieval church music practice which trickled down to the folk tradition or whether it is an example of ancient and generally forgotten folk practice which in the Middle Ages was taken up by the Western church. Today the interest in primacy has dwindled, especially as various kinds of polyphony have been discovered in many European folk traditions, but we may still marvel at what must surely be a musical tradition of great age. Aside from simple parallel fifths, Icelandic music seems to have used other forms similar to the earliest polyphony in Western church music, such as the so-called free and melismatic types of organum.

There is no doubt that many of the folk dances of Europe were originally dances of medieval and later towns and courts. This is true of the square dances, which grew out of the quadrilles; of the polka, once a more stately dance; and of the waltz, which originated in part in the slower and more dignified minuet. Frequently, of course, the dance almost completely changed character when it moved from court to countryside and vice-versa. Thus the sarabande, one of the slowest and most stately dances of seventeenth-century Western Europe, is thought to have been derived from a Spanish folk dance which, in turn, was brought from the Spanish-American colonies in the sixteenth century and was quick and violent. More rarely, the music accompanying folk dances can also be traced to earlier forms of art music. In such cases we have musical instances of *gesunkenes*

Kulturgut. Examples can be found in Sweden, where one of the important folk dances is the "polska," which is a form of the polonaise. Anyone familiar with Chopin's polonaises will recognize the characteristic rhythm in Example 4-8, which is played by violins. Aside from rhythm, however, the melodic configurations are definitely also in a style reminiscent of baroque and pre-Classical music: the arpeggios and the triad-like figures in the second section, reminiscent of the Alberti bass. The form, in which each phrase is repeated with first and second endings, is common in Western European instrumental music and similar also to the earliest known examples of medieval instrumental music, the *estampie* or *stantipes*. Only the melodic line—not the accompaniment—is given in Example 4-8.

EXAMPLE 4-8. Swedish "Polska" played by two violins; melody only, transcribed by Bruno Nettl from recording issued by Sveriges Radio (Radio Sweden), RAEP 8. Collected in Halsingsland.

Tunes of various sorts, frequently more ornamented, are played in other Scandinavian countries on instruments such as the Norwegian "Harding fiddle." Typical of the multifarious forms of folk instruments in Europe, this is a violin with four or five sympathetic strings under the finger board (which are not played but are caused to vibrate by the vibrations of those strings which are activated by the bow). The four main strings are tuned in various ways, for example , , or .

Swedish Dulcimer.

Another instrument prominent in Scandinavia is the dulcimer, which in Sweden exists in a great many forms. Unlike the dulcimer of the Southern United States, it is used more as a solo instrument than as an accompaniment to singing. It produces melodies with drone accompaniments, or tunes in parallel thirds. The dulcimer, basically, is a string instrument that lies flat on a table and is plucked; it has anywhere from three to over a dozen strings, and usually one or more of the strings are fretted. The shape varies from that of an oblong violin to rectangular and irregularly triangular. Sometimes it is bowed as well as plucked. It seems likely that the American dulcimer was brought from Scandinavia or Northern Germany, though similar instruments do, of course, exist elsewhere in Europe.

Throughout Europe, folk music enthusiasts are deploring the gradual disappearance of folk singing and the knowledge of folk music on the part of the rural population. Attempts to reintroduce folk music through schools and festivals have been only moderately successful. Nevertheless, there still seem to be many people who know and can sing folk songs from their family or village traditions. Denmark seems to be such a place, for we have available in a case study, made over a period of time by the Danish musicologist Nils Schiørring,[8] all of the songs known by one woman, Selma Nielsen. Mrs. Nielsen produced some 150 songs from her memory, including material of very diverse origin—ballads from the Middle Ages, sea shanties, soldiers' songs, humorous ditties. It is possible to see throughout her repertory the close relationship between the development of folk and art music, for we find modal materials, jaunty songs in major and somewhat in the style of the lighter art songs of the pre-Classical period, and sentimental tunes obviously from nineteenth-century popular music. Scandinavia offers good illustrations of the interdependence of folk and art music in Europe.

German folk song

Nowhere is the interrelationship between art and folk music stronger than in the German-speaking nations. The influence of the sophisticated musician on his rural counterpart has sometimes been so great there that the old practices of the German countryside seem

[8] Nils Schiørring, *Selma Nielsens Viser* (Copenhagen: Munksgaard, 1956).

to have disappeared and can be traced only through old documents or through the music of Germans whose ancestors emigrated from their homeland centuries ago. This is analogous, of course, to the study of British folk music through American folk song. Germany does, however, have a body of folk songs rather similar in content to the English—medieval ballads, work songs, sailors' shanties, dances, year- and life-cycle songs, and so forth. In Germany proper, the vocal music seems to have developed much more strongly than the instrumental. But in Switzerland and Austria, instruments as well as special forms of singing have flourished. In the period since World War II, the emigrants from German-speaking communities in Hungary, the Balkans, and parts of Russia who returned to West Germany after centuries of isolation have produced singing informants with a knowledge of many older songs thought to have disappeared from the tradition.

The influence of the church on German folk song is of early medieval origin. Many of the German ballads with medieval themes have words of partly or entirely religious character. There are folkloric descendants of mystery plays in the modern moralities and in children's religious pageants. Much of the music fits in with the system of church modes as well as with the rhythmic structure of the early Lutheran hymns. The singing style is more frequently tempo-giusto than it is in the oldest British ballads. Typical of German ballad plots is the story of the merchant who gambles his son's life away. The boy's sister is told by the judge that she can redeem him by running around the gallows naked nine times, and she does this and saves her brother. We are reminded of "The Maid Freed from the Gallows" (Child 95), in which the maid's parents refuse to pay the maid's fee to redeem her, but her true love finally comes and does.

If the music of some of the old German ballads has medieval roots, the majority of extant German folk songs seem to stem from a later period, from the time—beginning in the seventeenth century—when the German countryside was dotted with minor courts each of which had a sophisticated musical life, with court composers, orchestras, and opera. In this way even the smallest hamlets and the most remote farms began to have contact with art music, and the result seems to have been the assimilation of elements of the art styles into folklore. The folk music from that period, typically, is in major and has melodies making liberal use of triads with implied harmony. Tempi and meters are even and constant, and the singing style is definitely tempo-giusto. There is also a later layer of song, that of the German broadside ballads, mainly from the nineteenth century. Here the style is that of nineteenth-century popular music, with some chromaticism, modulation, instrumental accompaniment, and what we today feel is a sentimental quality.

A children's song still widely used is shown in Example 4-9. It is sung in autumn by children while walking in pairs or small groups, carrying lanterns. The structure, which consists essentially of one

EXAMPLE 4-9. German children's song, "Laterne, Laterne," from pamphlet accompanying the recording, *Deutsche Volkslieder, eine Dokumentation des Deutschen Musikrates*, ed. Deutsches Volksliedarchiv, Freiburg (Wolfenbuttel: Moseler Verlag, 1961), p. 19.

line repeated with variations, is typical of children's songs throughout Europe and may, historically, represent an archaic layer of style that preceded the various national folk styles, which are evidently mainly of medieval origin. Especially typical is the scale, which is tetratonic, but which emphasizes the tones, E, G, and A. The added C in Example 4-9 may be interpreted as a result of the importance of the triad in German folk song style.

Polyphonic singing is not common in the Germanic-speaking nations, except for Germany, Austria, and Switzerland. Canons are found throughout Europe, but another characteristic form of polyphony in Germany is parallelism, particularly parallel thirds. Whether this came about through the influence of art music or whether it originated as a folk practice cannot be said. Perhaps it was once exclusively a folk practice that was reinforced by similar forms in art music. Much of the part-singing (which is concentrated in Southern Germany and the Alpine region) is definitely in the category of chordal harmony. This is surely the case in Example 4-10, a wood-

EXAMPLE 4-10. German woodsmen's song, from pamphlet accompanying the recording, *Deutsche Volkslieder, eine Dokumentation des Deutschen Musikrates*, ed. Deutsches Volksliedarchiv, Freiburg (Wolfenbüttel: Moseler Verlag, 1961), p. 11.

cutters' song from Bavaria. But at one point it leaves the widely accepted art music tradition: line 4 has several parallel fifths, which are performed consistently stanza after stanza. This song also, of course, indicates the importance, in German folk song, of triads in both harmony and melody.

German folk music outside Germany proper

The Alpine region of South Germany, Austria, and Switzerland has developed a regional body of folklore and folk music, including certain unique practices, which contrast with those of Germany proper. It is sometimes thought that the extreme isolation of the mountain dwellers as well as their exceptional physical environment are responsible for this regional peculiarity, and some scholars have tried to draw parallels between Alpine folklore and that of other mountain regions in the belief that geography plays an important role in determining the nature of a people's traditions. Two characteristic aspects of the Alpine musical heritage are the *alphorn* and yodeling.

The *alphorn* is a Swiss instrument, a wooden trumpet from four to twelve feet long, used to call cattle and to signal across valleys; it is played also at sunset rites. Similar instruments are found in other countries, including Estonia, Poland, and Rumania. Its repertory is mostly short calls, but there are also a few traditional tunes. Since its sound can be heard for miles, especially with the help of echoes, its presence in the Alps can be explained, at least partly, by the geographic environment. The fact that the player uses the higher partials has caused its music to make use of a peculiar scale—C-D-E-F sharp-G (transposed, of course, to various pitches when the instrument varies in size)—which has also been used as the basis of some Swiss folk songs.

Yodeling, the rapid alternation between chest and head voice while singing meaningless syllables, is also a practice due partly to the possibility of communicating over long distance from one mountainside to another. While we do find the use of falsetto in various continents, true yodeling is rare outside the Alpine region. Yodeling usually appears in the refrains of songs, although there are also some songs which consist entirely of yodeling. There is in the Alps also some polyphonic yodeling with parallel thirds or triads, for polyphonic singing of the type described for Germany is particularly strong in the Alps. The practice of yodeling has caused the emergence of a class of semiprofessional musicians in the Alpine region, for there are certain individuals who achieve fame as yodelers and who give paid performances.

Brief mention of European Jewish folk music is perhaps suitable in this section. The Yiddish folksongs are related to German folklore, for Yiddish is essentially a German dialect of the late Middle Ages that has been penetrated by loan words from Hebrew, Polish, Russian, and other languages. During the late Middle Ages, the Jews were driven out of Germany and sought refuge in Eastern Europe, keeping their special brand of German folk culture. Thus the songs of the Yiddish-speaking Jews have retained some of the German medieval character. But to a greater degree their songs partake of the styles of the nations to which they moved—Russia, Poland, Rumania, etc. And there are also traces of Hebrew liturgical music in their folk songs. Thus, the styles of Yiddish folk song have great variety, and the whole corpus of Yiddish folk music is not a homogeneous one. A similar development, incidentally, occurred in the case of the Sephardic Jews who, during the Middle Ages, lived in Spain but were driven out in 1492 and carried with them a Spanish-derived language, Ladino, and songs partially Spanish in style. (For a discussion of Israeli folk music, see William P. Malm's book in this series, *Music Cultures of the Pacific, the Near East, and Asia.*)

The mixture of German and East European elements that we find in Yiddish folk music is an appropriate stepping-stone to a discussion of Eastern European folk music. For while some of the Germanic-speaking peoples have close ties with the Romance-speaking cultures of Western Europe, there is also a great deal of interchange between Germans and Scandinavians on the one hand and Russians, Poles, Ukrainians, Hungarians, Czechs, and Yugoslavs on the other.

Bibliography and discography

Cecil J. Sharp is the author of a number of fundamental works on British folk music. One of his important works is *English Folk Song, Some Conclusions*, 3rd ed. (London: Methuen, 1954). A readable survey of the British ballad is Evelyn Wells, *The Ballad Tree* (New York:

Ronald Press, 1950). The most comprehensive collection of British ballad tunes, because it reprints the tunes in many other important collections, is Bertrand H. Bronson, *The Traditional Tunes of the Child Ballads* (Princeton, N.J.: Princeton University Press, 1958–), to be completed in four volumes. Bronson's article, "About the Commonest British Ballads" *J-IFMC*, IX (1957), 22-27, is important reading. Donal J. O'Sullivan, *Songs of the Irish* (New York: Crown Publishers, 1960) is a standard collection.

A short survey, with examples, of Dutch folk music is Jaap Kunst, "On Dutch Folk Dances and Dance Tunes," *Studies in Ethnomusicology*, I (1961), 29-37. For Norwegian folk music, a monumental set of volumes covering the entire repertory is being published under Olav Gurvin, *Norwegian Folk Music* (Olso: Oslo University Press, 1958–).

An interesting collection of Danish folk music collected from one informant is Nils Schiørring, *Selma Nielsens Viser* (Copenhagen: Munksgaard, 1956). Many collections of German folk music are available. A classic is Ludwig Erk and Franz Magnus Boehme, *Deutscher Liederhort* (Leipzig, 1893-1894, reprinted by Olms, Hildesheim, 1962). A more recent publication, still incomplete, but with comprehensive notes, is *Deutsche Volkslieder mit ihren Melodien*, edited by John Meier and others (Freiburg: Deutsches Volksliedarchiv, 1935–). Many publications by German scholars on German folk song are worth reading; those by Walter Wiora and Erich Stockmann are particularly to be noted. In the field of musical instruments, Stig Walin, *Die schwedische Hummel* (Stockholm: Nordiska Museet, 1952) is an excellent, profusely illustrated study of the Swedish dulcimer.

The number of records of British folk song, both field collections and artistic interpretations, is enormous. To be mentioned especially is a set of Child ballads produced by British traditional singers A. L. Lloyd and Ewan MacColl for class and other educational use, *English and Scottish Popular Ballads*, Washington Records 715-723. Also worth hearing are *Sussex Folk Songs and Ballads*, edited by Kenneth Goldstein, Folkways FG 3515; *Songs and Pipes of the Hebrides*, Folkways P 430; *The Art of the Bagpipe* (with elaborate annotations), Folk-Lyric Records FL 112; and, as a selection of Gaelic songs, *Songs of Aran*, Folkways P 1002.

Songs and Dances of Holland, Folkways 3576, and *Songs and Dances of Norway*, Folkways FE 4008, are both educational and entertaining selections. For German folk song, a set produced by the famous Freiburg archive is to be recommended: *Deutsche Volkslieder*, Deutsche Grammophongesellschaft 004-157 to 004-160 (2 disks), with a pamphlet giving texts, notes, and complete transcriptions.

5

Eastern Europe

If the area east of Italy, Germany, and Scandinavia has any internal unity in its folk music style, this must be due to the fact that the area, on the whole, has been much less under the influence of art music than has the western half of Europe. Peoples as diverse as the Greeks, the Russians, and the Finns can hardly be expected to have one style of folk music. For many centuries, parts of Eastern Europe have repeatedly been conquered by and re-conquered from several peoples from the outside—Mongols, Turks, Romans, Germans. Its culture has many roots, among them the Hellenistic, Islamic, Oriental, and North Asian. It is inhabited by peoples speaking languages of several distinct families and groups: Slavic, the largest group; Finno-

Ugric (Finnish, Hungarian, Estonian, and several minority languages in Russia); Turkic (the Turks, the Chuvash of the Russian interior, etc.); Romance (Rumanian); Albanian; and Caucasian. Musical influences come from sources as diverse as the chants of the Byzantine Church, the pentatonic tunes of Mongolia, and the complex rhythms of the Arabic and Hindu spheres. And certainly there are also important links between Eastern and Western Europe, tunes found in both areas, identical uses and functions of music in the culture. In view of this great diversity, we must be forgiven for selecting a few samples to characterize the area, and for omitting entirely consideration of some nations. But let us bear in mind that each of the Eastern European countries, from gigantic Russia to tiny Albania, has a rich folk music heritage; each has enough songs to fill a multi-volume anthology and a musical culture of sufficient wealth to keep scholars busy for several lifetimes.

Melodic sequence: Hungarians, Czechs, Cheremis

East European scholars have indeed been busy studying their native traditions, and nowhere has this been more true than in Hungary. For decades in the nineteenth century it was thought that the folk music of Hungary was the music of the gypsies who supplied ethnic entertainment in the cities, and not until the twentieth century was the great wealth of true Hungarian peasant music (which has little in common with the gypsy tunes) discovered, largely by Béla Bartók and Zoltán Kodály. Since the Hungarians are linguistically related to the Finns, it was thought that the styles of these two peoples would have something in common. This turned out to be only partially the case, but other Finno-Ugric speaking peoples living for centuries in isolation from the Hungarians, inside Russia, do have music somewhat similar to that of Hungary. The most important of these groups is the Cheremis, who live in a semi-autonomous republic of the USSR some five hundred miles east of Moscow. These peoples have something in common that is also found far to the east, among the Mongolians, and even to some extent further on, in American Indian music; and this strengthens our belief that the essential features of the oldest Hungarian folk music are very old, and that they were brought by the Finno-Ugric tribes when they moved westward in the early Middle Ages.

The most striking of these features is the practice of transposing a bit of melody several times to create the essence of a song. Many Hungarian songs have the form $A^1A^2A^1$(a fifth lower)A^2(a fifth lower), for example. Transposition is usually up or down a fifth, perhaps because this interval is an important one in the series of overtones, or perhaps because this practice may have originated long ago, in the Far East, under the influence of Chinese musical theory in which the fifth is significant, or for any of various reasons. In Hungarian folk music and even more in that of the Cheremis, pentatonic scales composed of major seconds and minor thirds are important. Such scales have sometimes been called "gapped scales" on the assumption that they are simply diatonic scales in which gaps have been made or left. Of course such a label is not really justified, for there is nothing any more "natural" about a scale made up of seconds (of two sizes) than there is about one made up of seconds and thirds,

EXAMPLE 5-1. Cheremis song, from Bruno Nettl, *Cheremis Musical Styles* (Bloomington: Indiana University Press, 1960), p. 37.

or, for that matter, one made up of quarter tones or augmented fourths. To demonstrate the integrity of the kind of pentatonic scale we have mentioned, let us examine a Cheremis song that makes use of the principle of transposition, in Example 5-1.

First we assign to each of the notes in the scale a number: beginning with the lowest tone, B—1, C sharp—2, E—3, F sharp—4, G sharp—5, B—6, C sharp—7, E—8. Then we compare the section labeled A with that labeled A^5. Obviously their melodic contours are similar, but at some of the points at which A has a minor third, A^5 has a major second, and A^5 begins a minor sixth below A but ends on a perfect fifth below A. Now, if we translate the tones into the numbers we have assigned, and compare musical lines A and A^5, we have the following sequences:

Line A^5 5 5 4 5 4 3 2 3 3 2 3 2 1
Line A 8 8 7 8 7 6 5 6 6 5 6 5 4.

The relationship between the number sequences is constant because, of course, the principle involved in this transposition is not a constant relationship of the vibration rates, which is what would occur if the interval of transposition were an exact one, but that of tonal transposition. Presumably the scale used in this song existed, in an unconscious sense, in the mind of the composer when he was making up the song, and when he began transposing he did so within the framework of the scale, which is made up of both thirds and seconds.

The practice of transposing as an integral part of the composition process seems to have radiated from Hungary to its neighbor

EXAMPLE 5-2. Czech folk song, "Vrt sa devca," learned by the author from oral tradition.

countries. The Slovaks and, to a smaller extent, the Czechs make use of it also. The Slovaks transpose sections largely in the manner of the Hungarians (up or down a fifth), but the Czechs do this more frequently to the intervals of the third or second. Perhaps the difference between the Czechs and Hungarians here is due to the greater frequency of diatonic, especially of major scales, among the Czechs. Again, the influence of neighbor nations may be at work, for the Czechs have lived in an area surrounded by Germans and they participated, more than their neighbors to the east, in the development of art music. Thus their songs sound more like Western cultivated music, and they have variants of many tunes found also in Germany. Example 5-2 is a Czech song using transposition.

Words, music, and rhythm: The Balkans and Czechoslovakia

It is interesting to compare the rhythmic structures of the Czech and German folk songs. That of the Czech songs frequently is more accented, while the German flows more smoothly. The German songs more frequently have an anacrusis—pickup or up-beat, as it is popularly called—while the Czech ones rarely do. This may be related to one of the differences between the two languages. Czech speakers tend to accent their stressed syllables heavily, and the Czech language automatically places an accent on the first syllable of each word. Also, Czech has no articles such as "a" or "the" that would be unstressed. As a result, Czech speech is so constructed that utterances begin with accents, and so do Czech songs and instrumental folk compositions. German, with its accents coming on any syllable, and with its unstressed articles preceding the nouns, has given rise to a musical structure in which an unstressed beat in the music often precedes the first measure. Of course we could not claim that the rhythmic structure of a folk music style automatically comes from the language, and we could easily find examples in which the rhythm of folk songs contravenes that of their language. However, there is no doubt that the nature of a language has much to do with shaping the style of the folk songs for which it is used.

The Czech folk songs include many that deal with agricultural life, and these are among the most popular. They are usually not real work songs, but lyrical poems sung after work. A few examples are given here in English:[1]

[1] Czech folk song texts quoted from Bruno Nettl and Ivo Moravcik, "Czech and Slovak Folk Songs Collected in Detroit," *Midwest Folklore* V (1955), 40-48.

Around Trebon, around Trebon
Horses are grazing on the lord's field.
Give the horses, I'm telling you,
Give the horses oats.
When they have had their fill
They will carry me home.

Often they concern love among young peasants. For example:—

Come, young man, to our house in the morning.
You shall see what I do.
I get up in the morning, I water the cows,
And I drive the sheep to pasture.

The fruits of agriculture may be used as special symbols in the text:—

Under the oak, behind the oak
She had one or two
Red apples; she gave one to me.
She did not want to give me both,
She began to make excuses,
That she hasn't, that she won't give, that there are too few.

Many of the Czech lyrical songs deal with or mention music, such as this—

In the master's meadow I found a ducat.
Who will change it for me? My sweetheart is not at home.
If she won't change it I'll give it to the cimbal (dulcimer) player.
The music will play until dawn.

The rhythm of Czech and Slovak songs is relatively simple, with the meters typically an isometric duple or triple. Hungarian folk songs are frequently in similarly simple meter, but there are also many Hungarian songs with irregular metric patterns, and some that move steadily in 5/4 or 7/4 meter. One of the common features of Hungarian rhythm is the use of dotted figures— ♩. ♪ or, even more typically, ♪♩.—with heavy stress on the first note. Perhaps, again, the rhythmic structure of the language is evident here, for in Hungarian, as in Czech, there are no articles, and the first syllable is automatically accented. Also common in Hungarian and some other Eastern European folk styles is the use of isorhythmic structure. This means that a rhythmic pattern is repeated for each line. The meters may vary and the measures may have irregular numbers of beats, but the sequence of note values remains the same from line to line in this type of song. The following rhythmic patterns appear in some of the Hungarian as well as the Rumanian folk songs with isorhythmic structure:

The reason for the frequency of this kind of structure in some Eastern European styles may lie, again, in the structure of the poetry. In Western Europe, it is the number of metric feet (iambic, trochaic, dactyllic, anapestic) which are constant. Each foot corresponds to one or to a half measure of music. The actual number of syllables per line may vary, since a line consisting of iambic feet may suddenly be broken by a foot of anapest:

"*There was a youth and a jol-ly youth*" ("and a jol-" is the anapest foot).

But in most Eastern European styles of poetry it is not the number of accented syllables that is constant, but the number of syllables in toto. Thus an isorhythmic arrangement, even if each phrase has several measures of different lengths, is better for accommodating the kind of line sequence that makes up the poetry.

On the whole, the Balkan countries have in common an unusual degree of rhythmic complexity. It appears in three forms: 1) freely declaimed melodies, which can only with difficulty be classified as to meter, and which are performed with extremes of the parlando-rubato technique; 2) tunes with few different note values, but with frequently changing meter; and 3) tunes with a single dominant meter which, however, is based on a prime number of beats—5, 7, 11, 13, and so on. The first type is well exemplified in the Yugoslav epic, which is discussed below in this chapter. The second and third types are especially common in the Rumanian and Bulgarian traditions, so much so that songs in 11/8 or 7/8 have been called tunes "in Bulgarian rhythm" among Balkan folk song scholars. Example 5-3 gives some of the rhythms found in these songs.

Example 5-4 is a Rumanian Christmas carol with the meter of 10/16 kept consistently throughout the song. Actually it might be possible to divide the song into measures of different lengths, but in spite of the rather complicated relationship between such note values as eighths and dotted eighths, or sixteenths and dotted sixteenths,

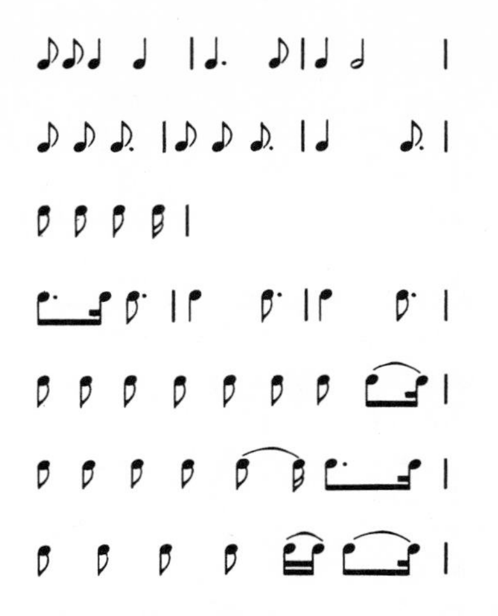

EXAMPLE 5-3. Examples of metric patterns found in Bulgarian folk songs.

there is a steady rhythmic pulse which is followed throughout: ♪ ♪. ♪. ♪. The curious thing is that the pulse is not regular. It alternates between eighths and dotted eights. Perhaps this is the key to the rhythmic complexity of some Balkan songs; there is a meter—10/16 in this case—but the denominator of the fraction does not in-

EXAMPLE 5-4. Rumanian Christmas Carol, from Béla Bartók, *Die Melodien der rumanischen Colinde* (Wien: Universal Edition, 1935), p. 68. Reprinted by permission of Boosey and Hawkes, Inc., New York, and Universal Edition, Ltd., London. Copyright 1918 by Universal Edition, Renewed 1945. Copyright and renewal assigned to Boosey and Hawkes, Inc., for U.S.A.

dicate the length of the beat, as it would in most Western European music, because the beat is not of the same length but varies, depending on its position in the measure.

It would seem almost that ♪♪. ♪. ♪. is another version of ♪♪♪♪. and that ♬♬. is simply an elongation of a simpler figure, ♬♬. We should point out, incidentally, that there is a vast body of Christmas carols in the Rumanian folk repertory. Bartók collected several hundred tunes, and they seem to be particularly archaic melodies, being short, with forms that do not correspond to the simple line organization of Western European, Czech, or Hungarian songs, but which are irregular not only in the structure of the measures but also in the number of measures and phrases per song.

One might expect the dances of the Balkan countries to be more prone to simple metric schemes; after all, people have two legs and two arms, which lend themselves well to the movement in duple meter; no one has seven feet. Nevertheless, among the five most important folk dances of the Bulgarians, only one is in duple meter. The Bulgarians have 1) the *Pravo Horo*, simple round dance, in 2/4 meter; 2) the *Paiduška,* in quintuple meter, with two beats— ♩ ♩. ; 3) the *Povărnato Horo*, back-and-forth round dance, in 9/16, with four beats—♪ ♪ ♪ ♪. ; 4) *Račenica,* danced by couples in 7/8 meter, with three beats–♩ ♩ ♩.; and 5) *Eleno mome* ("My Helen"), a more recent introduction, also in 7/8, with four beats—♩ ♩ ♪ ♩. The metric structure of these dances, once established, is quite consistent.

EXAMPLE 5-5. Rumanian Christmas Carol, from Béla Bartók, *Die Melodien der rumanischen Colinde* (Wien: Universal Edition, 1935), p. 43. Reprinted by permission of Boosey and Hawkes, Inc., New York, and Universal Edition, Ltd., London. Copyright 1918 by Universal Edition, renewed 1945. Copyright and renewal assigned to Boosey and Hawkes, Inc., for U.S.A.

The tunes with the meter frequently changing are illustrated by Example 5-5, a simple Rumanian Christmas carol with the range of a sixth, with alternation among 3/8, 4/8, and 5/8, and, except for the repetition of the first rhythmic phrase at the end, no recurring metric scheme. This song also illustrates the simple yet irregular structure of some of the Balkan songs. It could be described by the letter scheme ABA, although A and B are not of the same length.

Form in Balkan folk songs

The forms of the Balkan songs do exhibit considerable differences from those of Western Europe. In the latter area, we are overwhelmed by a large number of four-line stanzas, in which we have either progressive developments (ABCD, each line a new melody with no repetition) or some recurrence of the first line. AABA is very common in German folk music, in the British broadsides, and in modern popular and popular-derived songs. ABBA is common also in the older British ballads, especially in relationship to the curved melodic contour. The reverting forms—AABA and ABBA—are common also in the western part of Eastern Europe, in Czech, Polish, and Hungarian song. AABA especially is found in Czech and Polish music, perhaps because of strong German influence. ABBA is found in Hungarian and other Finno-Ugric groups, but more common is a variant of this form, A A(5) A(5) A, indicating transposition of the first section up or down a fifth for the second and third sections. The use of three sections, such as ABA, with the middle section longer and at a tempo different from that of the first, as in Example 5-5, is sometimes found in the Balkans and also among the Czechs. Songs with two, five, and six or more lines are found throughout the Balkans and in the Baltic area. Often these can be subdivided into asymmetrical units (like the measures in Bulgarian rhythm). A common form in the Rumanian Christmas songs is ABCAC, a form divisible into two main parts, ABC and the somewhat truncated AC.

An area of the world as rich in both folk tunes and folk song scholars as the Balkans was perhaps bound to produce pioneer work in the classification of musical forms. Bartók devised a system which he used for his collections of Hungarian, Slovak, Rumanian, and

Serbo-Croatian songs. In his Slovak collection, the songs are first divided according to the number of melodic lines (normally two, three, or four) without counting repetitions of material. Thus a tune with the form ABBA has two different melodic lines, but the form ABCD has four. Each class is then subdivided according to the position of the final tones of the lines in their relationship to the last tone of the song. For example, a song in which all lines end on the same pitch is in one class; one in which the sequence of final tones of lines is GAAG would be in another; and so on. Beyond this, each of the categories is then divided according to rhythm–dotted rhythms are separated from even rhythms. Finally, each of these groups is subdivided according to the number of syllables per line, distinguishing the songs that have the same number of syllables in in each line from those in which the number varies from line to line. Bartók's scheme of classifying melodies differs greatly, however, from that used by most students of British folk song, such as Cecil Sharp, who classified tunes according to mode. The reason for this difference is probably related to the fact that there is in the British (and other Western European) styles less formal variety than there is in East European folk music, for the former, being based on poetry with metric feet, relies on more or less constant meter and length of line.

Epics: Yugoslavia, Finland, Russia

If we measured the intonation of genuine folk singers anywhere we would probably find that their intervals do not coincide as well with those in standard music theory as our notations indicate. Especially in Eastern Europe, and perhaps more in the Balkans than elsewhere, would we find intervals smaller than the minor second, thirds which are neither major nor minor, and the like. The Balkans have for centuries been under the cultural influence–now strong, now weaker–of the Near East, where small intervals are common. But they have also conformed to a degree with the diatonic system found in Western folk and art music, and with the widespread pentatonic modes which use minor thirds and major seconds and can be derived from the circle of fifths. Thus we find a great deal of variety in the melodic material used in Balkan folk music. An interesting example of scales and intervals quite unusual in Western Europe is the large body of heroic epic song in Yugoslavia.

Actually, the tradition of epic poetry is quite widespread in Europe. An epic can be defined as a narrative poem, usually sung, with a heroic main character, a number of events, wars and battles, considerable length (this varies greatly, of course, but an epic is normally distinctly longer than a ballad), and a form whose point of orientation is the single line rather than the stanza. In the Middle Ages the epic was fairly widespread in Western Europe; the French "chansons de geste" and such famous works as the "Song of Roland" are examples. In Western Europe, the epic tradition was evidently one in which folk and sophisticated traditions shared and mixed, for it was presumably carried by professional minstrels who at least partially used written texts. In Eastern Europe the epic tradition is today much more alive and much more closely associated with the genuine folk culture. We find epic material in the Slavic world, but also in Albania and Finland, where the main body of folk epics, the *Kalevala*, consists of songs dealing with the Finnish mythical culture hero, Väinemöinen. The *Kalevala* is structured in couplets, and the songs were performed by pairs of bards who would alternate, which is probably responsible for the peculiarly repetitive form of the text shown in this excerpt:[2]

O thou wisest Väinemöinen,
O thou oldest of magicians,
Speak thy words of magic backwards,
And reverse thy songs of magic.
Loose me from this place of terror
And release me from my torment.

Of course the reader will recognize the style as that also used in Longfellow's "Song of Hiawatha." The influence of the *Kalevala* on nineteenth-century poets was certainly considerable. The Finnish bards used the accompaniment of the *kantele*, a psaltery with 20 to 30 strings.

The Russian tradition of epic poetry is, typically, unaccompanied. The Russian poems are called *byliny;* they are slow-moving, unrimed, and performed in a rhythmically free style. Their stories—in contrast to the mythical past of the Finnish *Kalevala* cycle—deal with historical or semihistorical events of eleventh-century Russia

[2] *Kalevala, the Land of the Heroes* (New York: Dutton, 1907) I, 29.

and of the wars against the Tartars which took place for the next two hundred years. Of course there are literary motifs that are found in many nations: for instance, the poor and neglected prince who becomes a hero, found in all European folklore but perhaps without historical foundation. The practice of singing *byliny* seems to have reached a peak of artistic perfection in the seventeenth century, when it was—as was the epic tradition of Western Europe in the Middle Ages—penetrated by professional minstrels. The Ukrainian version of the epic is a body of songs called *Dumy*, dealing largely with the struggles of the Ukrainians against the Tartars and Poles in the late Middle Ages.

The most accessible body of epic singing today, however, is that of the Yugoslavs (mainly the Serbs, but also the Croatians, Montenegrins, Bulgarians, and Albanians). Their songs deal mainly with the struggles against the Turks from the thirteenth to the seventeenth centuries. Some of the epics are told from the Christian point of view, but others, from the Muslim. The songs deal mainly with the rulers and the leaders in war. That the tradition is still alive is attested by the mention of modern appliances such as the telephone, and by the existence of an epic about the shooting of Archduke Ferdinand at Sarajevo at the beginning of World War I. That it is also ancient is proved by its musical structure. There have been attempts to link the Yugoslav tradition to that of the Greek Homeric epics, and certainly we can learn a great deal about what may have been the genesis of the *Iliad* and *Odyssey* and about the way in which these great epics must have been performed from the structure and cultural context of the Yugoslav epics.

The Yugoslav epics last from less than one to perhaps ten hours, they are performed by semiprofessional minstrels in cafes, and they are sung only by men. They are accompanied on the *gusla* or *gusle* (which the singer himself plays), a simple fiddle with one string made of a strand of horsehair, a belly of stretched skin, and a crude bow. The *gusle* usually plays a more ornamented version of the singer's melody, or it performs a drone and plays ornaments between the singer's lines.

It would be surprising if songs of such length were sung exactly the same way by any two singers, or even twice by the same one. To some extent they must be improvised, re-created each time. Thus the process of creation and performance are to a degree united.

There are points where adherence to a norm is required, of course; a particular epic has certain themes, certain motifs, and certain formulae—similar to the "conceits" of the British ballads—which recur. In the structure, one of the typical arrangements is the ten-syllable line, which remains constant throughout the hours required to complete the poem. Just how a singer who is partly improvising can consistently and undeviatingly produce lines of exactly ten syllables is one of the mysteries of this ancient tradition. But even more exacting is the requirement of a word boundary after the fourth syllable in some of the Yugoslav styles; that is, the fourth syllable always ends a word, and no word occupies both syllables fourth and fifth. Here is a sample of this kind of poetry:[3]

Beg sađ priđe đamu đo penđera,
Pa dofati knjige i hartije,
Kaljem drvo što se knjiga gradi,
A mastila što se knjiga piše,
Pa načinje knjigu šarovitu,
Sprema knjigu ljićkom Mustajbegu.

(*Translation*): *Now the bey went to the window*
And he took letter paper,
A quill with which letters are made,
And ink with which letters are written,
And he prepared a well-writ letter,
He directed the letter to Mustajbey of the Lika.

Example 5-6 gives a short sample of the music, showing its very ornamental style of singing and playing, and including some small intervals. The scale could not be notated without the use of additional marks; arrows indicate slight (quarter-tone) raising or lowering. The notes played by the *gusle* include, consistently, a tone between C-flat and C, and one between G and G-sharp. Several possible reasons for this use of microtones have been advanced: the influence of Turkish and Arabic music; the ancient Greek tradition, with its enharmonic genus; and the use of the *gusle*, which, when fingered by the human hand in natural position of tension, produces such intervals.

The rhythm of Yugoslav epics is also worthy of discussion. If

[3] Albert B. Lord, *The Singer of Tales* (Cambridge, Mass.: Harvard University Press, 1960), p. 84.

EXAMPLE 5-6. Sample of Yugoslav epic song, from Milman Parry and Albert B. Lord, *Serbo Croatian Heroic Songs*, vol. 1 (Cambridge, Mass.: Harvard University Press, 1954), p. 440.

the many vocal ornaments were disregarded, we would find two main types:

♩ ♩ ♩ ♩ | ♩ ♩ ♩ ♩ | 𝅗𝅥 ♩ 𝄽 | and 𝅗𝅥 ♩ | ♩ ♩ ♩ | ♩ ♩ ♩ | ♩ ♩ 𝄽 |. But near the beginning of a song or an episode (usually preceded by introductions played on the *gusle*) the rhythm varies more, the first note of each line is elongated, and the singing has an even more dramatic character than it does in the remainder of the song.

Finally, we should point out that regional and individual styles of singing are very highly developed in Yugoslav epic poetry. Two singers will sing the same song with many points of difference. Albert Lord narrates an incident of great interest which affords unusual insight into the relationship of tradition and individual creativity:

> When [the epic collector and scholar Milman] Parry was working with the most talented Yugoslav singer in our experience, Avdo

Mededović in Bijelo Polje, he tried the following experiment. Avdo had been singing and dictating for weeks; he had shown his worth and was aware that we valued him highly. Another singer came to us, Mumin Vlahovljak from Plevlje. He seemed to be a good singer and he had in his repertory a song that Parry discovered was not known to Avdo; Avdo said he had never heard it before. Without telling Avdo that he would be asked to sing the song himself when Mumin had finished it, Parry set Mumin to singing, but he made sure that Avdo was in the room and listening. When the song came to an end, Avdo was asked his opinion of it and whether he could now sing it himself. He replied that it was a good song and that Mumin had sung it well, but that he thought he might sing it better. The song was a long one of several thousand lines. Avdo began and as he sang, the song lengthened, the ornamentation and richness accumulated, and the human touches of character, touches that distinguished Avdo from other singers, imparted a depth of feeling that had been missing in Mumin's version.[4]

Scales and intervals: Bulgaria, Greece, Poland

The use of small intervals—some microtones, but more frequently minor seconds—is an important feature of some Balkan styles outside the epic tradition. The importance of ornamentation seems to have contributed to this predilection, for vocal ornaments as well as instrumental ones seem especially made for the use of small intervals. Thus a Macedonian song uses a scale with the tones E-flat, D, C, B, and A-sharp. The fact that the ranges of Balkan songs are, typically, small may also be a contributing factor. According to Kremenliev,[5] Bulgarian songs rarely exceed an octave in range, and a great many of them are within the compass of a fifth. Occasionally one even finds two-tone melodies with only a minor second between the tones. Ornaments in Bulgarian folk song are improvised; they vary from stanza to stanza and, in one song, from singer to singer. Their purpose may be that of pleasing the audience through vocal virtuosity, of calling attention to the song or to particular words (this is evidently the purpose of melismatic passages preceding a song, a prac-

[4] Lord, *The Singer of Tales*, p. 78.

[5] Boris Kremenliev, *Bulgarian-Macedonian Folk Music* (Berkeley and Los Angeles: University of California Press, 1952), p. 78.

tice common also in the Yugoslav epics), or imitating instrumental passages.

Greek folk music, like that of some other Balkan countries, seems to be a combination of archaic and more recent melodies and contains a tremendous diversity of styles. It is possible to find traces of the ancient Greek modes, and many Greek songs fit perfectly into the system of the diatonic modes. Many other songs, however, are more chromatic. Perhaps the combination of these two concepts—diatonic modes with small, chromatic steps—is responsible for the existence of heptatonic scales that have four minor seconds, such as the so-called Gypsy scale: C-D-E flat-F sharp-G-A flat-B. In most ways, however, Greek folk music seems to show the influences of centuries of Turkish and Muslim occupation. What remains of the ancient Greek traits seems best preserved in Asia Minor and the islands of the Aegean.

One of the most interesting folk song types of the Greeks is the "Klephtic song." The Klephts (meaning bandits in Turkish) were the men who fought for Greek independence against the Turks from the fifteenth to the nineteenth centuries. Klephtic songs deal with these fighters, who have become folk heroes, in a way somewhat similar to that of the Yugoslav epics. These songs are performed in a rubato manner, with much ornamentation and complex metric arrangements. They do have a strophic structure, but the melodic and poetic forms do not coincide; in fact, the musical line ordinarily covers one and a half textual lines. Thus, in a sense the modern Greeks share in the epic traditions of Eastern Europe.

Polish folk music is quite different from that of the Balkans and also from that of the Czechs and Slovaks. It is more closely related to that of Russia. The oldest layer of songs is pentatonic, but the majority make use of seven-tone scales, which can be classed as church modes. Those modes similar to the minor mode, with lowered sixth and seventh or lowered third, are the most common; this is true also of Russian folk music. In contrast to Russia, Poland has little polyphonic folk music and what part-singing there is seems to be of recent origin and emphasizes parallel thirds. The range of the songs is relatively small. A peculiarity of the singing style—typical perhaps of many and varied peculiarities of singing through Europe that never seem to appear in the printed collections of folk songs—is the practice of holding the final note of a song for several seconds, or of trailing off with a downward glissando.

Musical instruments

Perhaps the most characteristic feature of East European folk music is its wealth of instruments and instrumental music. There are far too many instrument types to enumerate or describe, and again we must be content with a sampling. Instruments may serve as clues to the musical past of a nation or region. For example, the association between ancient Greek and modern Near Eastern and Slavic cultures is evident in their use of similar instruments. The ancient Greek *aulos* was a reed instrument with two tubes; similar instruments are today found among the Persians, Arabs, Turks, and Southern Slavs. In Yugoslavia, an instrument of this type is the *dvojnice* which is, in effect, a double recorder or plugged flute. The right-hand tube has, typically, four finger holes and is used for playing simple, embellished melodies; the left-hand side, then, has three holes and is normally used to play an accompanying drone.

The Czechs, Slovaks, and Hungarians also have a fine body of instrumental music. One of the most widely used instruments there is the bagpipe, which (perhaps to the surprise of some) is by no means limited to the British Isles; on the contrary, it is found throughout Europe and parts of Asia, and evidently it was brought to Scotland from the East.

The kinds of bagpipes found in various countries differ, of course, from the very simple kinds found among the semiliterate tribes in Russia (such as the Cheremis) to the beautifully fashioned and sonorous instruments with three and four pipes found in Western Europe. In Scottish and Irish piping, the tunes are most frequently unrelated to the vocal music, and complex compositional forms, such as *Pibroch*—a kind of theme with variations—make up the repertory. In Eastern Europe, however, much of the bagpipe music consists of the same tunes as are used in vocal music, and some Hungarian folk songs, for instance, appear—with richer ornamentation—in the bagpipe repertory.

Folk music instruments seem to be especially numerous in Poland. Many forms of several basic types—flutes, fiddles, bagpipes—exist, each with regional variants. For example, among the stringed instruments, there is a one-stringed *diable skrzypce* (devil's fiddle); a musical bow with three strings; several types of *gensle* (fiddles in

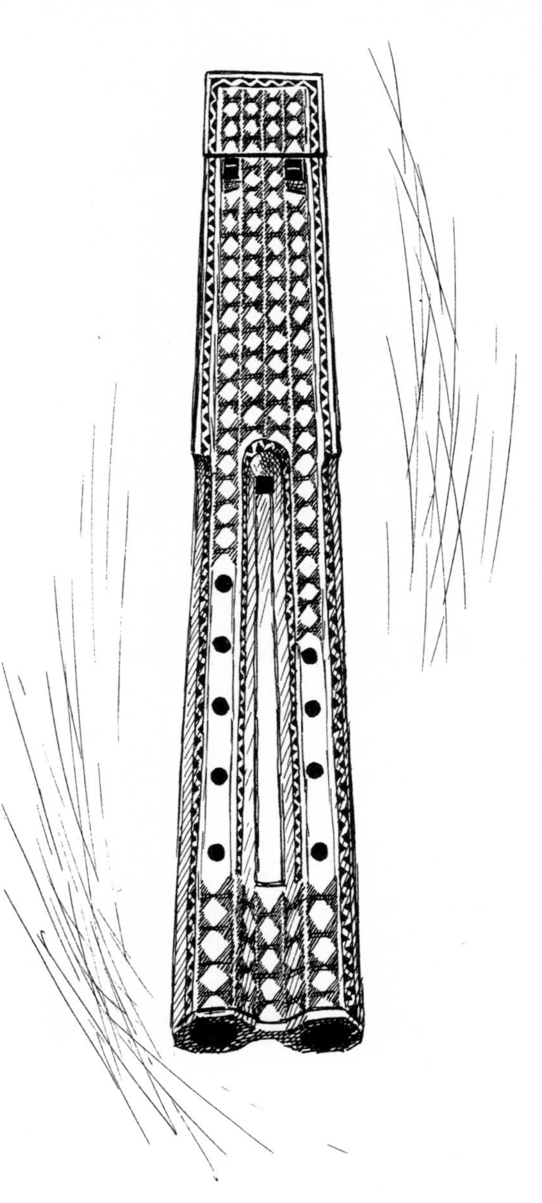

Yugoslav double recorder.

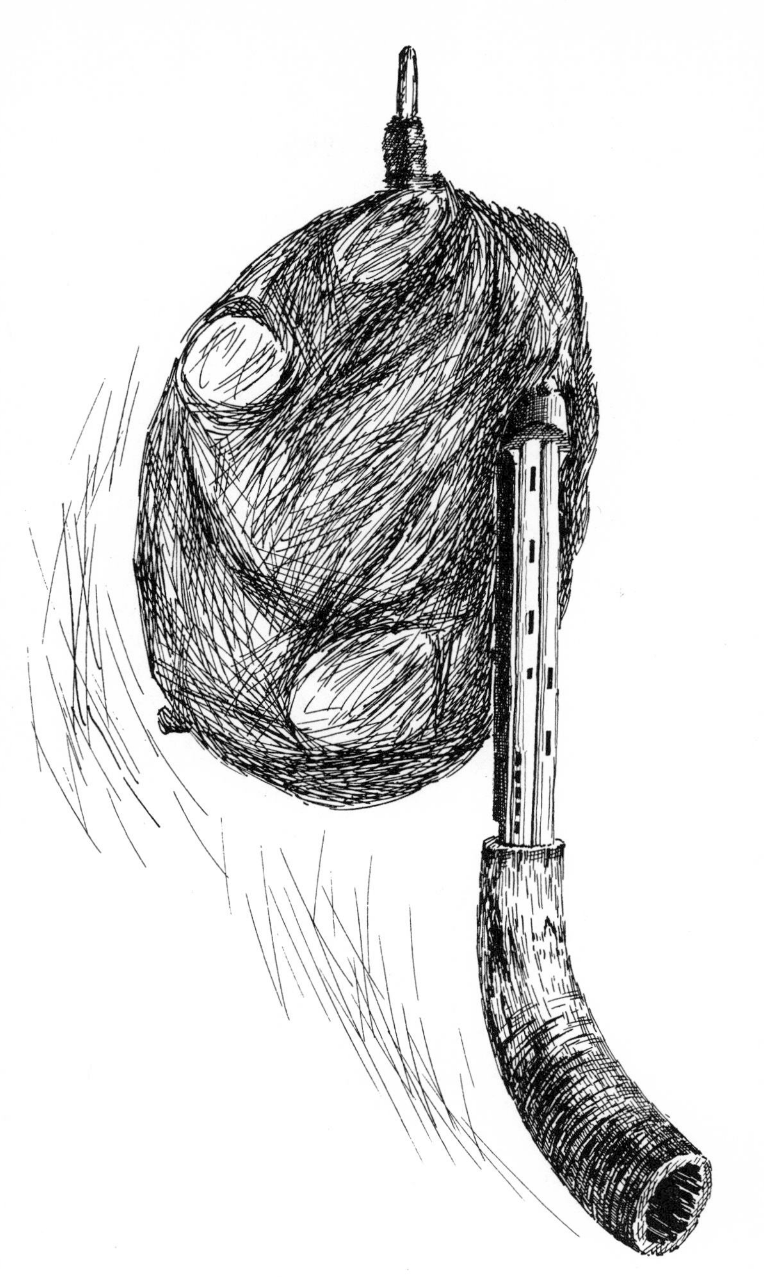

Cheremis bagpipe.

various shapes with four and five strings, some held on the knee, some under the chin; the *suka*, with four strings tuned in fifths; the *mazanka*, a small fiddle with three strings tuned in fifths; and the *maryna*, a very large fiddle, also with three strings tuned in fifths, a form of the medieval Western European *tromba marina*.

Perhaps because of the proliferation of instruments, Polish folk music is dominated by instrumental tunes, most of it, of course, used for dancing. There is an immense number of dance types, each with regional provenience. Some of these have been taken over into art music by composers such as Chopin—the polonaise, the mazurka, the polka, the krakowiak. Typically, the Polish dances are quick and the majority use triple meter.

Polyphony: The Slavic countries and the Caucasus

Polyphony is one element of music that characterizes all of Eastern Europe. It seems to exist everywhere except among the Finno-Ugric and Turkic peoples, and its development has been greatest in Russia and the Caucasus. The existence, among the Georgians, of polyphonic songs similar to the *organa* of medieval Europe has long tantalized the historian of Western art music, who can hardly assume that the Caucasus could have had an influence on Western European practices, and who finds the East too remote to have received stimuli of such a specific nature from the medieval West, but who also believes that the two forms may be too similar to have been invented independently twice. This is one of the riddles of historical ethnomusicology that may never be solved. The existence of organum-like folk music in Iceland and of other polyphonic types in Spain, Italy, and elsewhere (sporadically) indicates a possible solution: that polyphonic singing was once widespread in folk practice but receded to the marginal areas of Europe. Example 5-7 is a song of the Gur, a tribe in the Caucasus, in three voices. The solo phrase at the beginning is typical also of Russian and Ukrainian polyphony. The first part of the song makes liberal, though not consistent, use of parallel triads. The second part also uses the principle of the drone, above which parallel thirds appear.

The role of Eastern (Orthodox) Church music in the development of this kind of polyphony may have been considerable. Po-

EXAMPLE 5-7. Gurian polyphonic folk song, from Robert Lach, *Gesänge russischer Kriegsgefangener* Band 3, 1. Abt. (Wien: Wiener Akademie der Wissenschaften, 55. Mitteilung der Phonogrammarchivs Kommission, 1928), p. 108.

lyphony was officially adopted by the Eastern Church in the seventeenth century, and in Russian folk polyphony, although there are occasional parallel fifths, the tendency is to use four voices in triadic structure. In Russia and the Ukraine, the practice of polyphonic singing is extremely important. Singing is typically a group activity, except in the case of narrative poetry, and even in the 1950's we hear of young people in Russian cities walking in groups and singing informally. The polyphonic songs are traditional, but some improvisation in the lower parts seems to be acceptable. In the Russian songs, the upper voice is definitely the melody; but in the Ukrainian ones, the two or three voices seem to be roughly equal in importance. Parenthetically, we should point out the rather unusual developments in Russian folk music since World War I. The Soviet government has attempted to preserve the folk heritage not only of the Russians but also of some of the many minority populations in the Soviet Union, at the same time making their songs servants of the communist ideology. The result is a large body of folk song in the traditional musical styles—although the traits of Russian songs per se have to an extent penetrated the domain of some of the minority groups—with words of recent origin, often mentioning the leaders of the Soviet Union and the communist ideology.

The Cossacks of the Don River basin (who have produced the famous professional Don Cossack choruses) have developed the art of polyphonic singing to especially great heights; evidently even the epic *byliny* were sometimes sung by them in chorus. Another area of Russia in which polyphony flourishes is the North, especially the area around the monastery of Pečory. The Ukrainians also have a polyphonic style of great interest, and Example 5-8 is typical of those Ukrainian songs which make use of parallel fifths. The polyphony of the Eastern Slavs, while essentially relying on parallel move-

EXAMPLE 5-8. Ukrainian polyphonic song from Poltava, collected by Ossyp and Roman Rosdolsky, transcribed by Bruno Nettl.

ment, does not follow this principle throughout. There is occasional oblique and contrary motion, use of the drone and even of imitation. Nor does the interval between the voices remain constant in one song. Example 5-8 contains parallel fifths as well as parallel thirds, with occasional fourths and sixths. The beginning by a soloist is typical and the choral parts may be doubled at the octave when both men and women sing. Tonality, in the case of the parallel fifths, may be difficult to identify, for each voice retains its own distinct tonality in order to preserve strict parallelism. But a common closing formula that establishes the final tonality proceeds from a third or triad built on the second degree of the scale to an octave on the tonic.

As we move westward, polyphony decreases in prominence, and the vertical intervals become smaller. Poles, Czechs, and Slovaks use parallel thirds (and occasionally sixths), perhaps under the influence of the Alpine style with its emphasis on triadic harmony and melody. In the Balkans we also find vertical seconds and, occasionally, parallel seconds. In Yugoslavia there are some vertical seconds in the songs of lament, which employ a practice known as "Ojkanie" whose sound is rather similar to that of the epics. The members of the Balkan folk cultures evidently do not consider the harmonic seconds complex or difficult to perform, for in Bulgaria even children's songs can contain them.

Although polyphony is not common in the Baltic area, it does occur in some interesting forms using vertical seconds. Example 5-9 is a Lithuanian round, sung by three groups, in which only two tones are sung simultaneously. The reason is that one of the three groups is always resting. Thus, the tune, consisting of phrases A and B and the rest, X, has the following form when sung as a round:

Voice 1	A	B	X	A	B	X		
Voice 2		A	B	X	A	B		
Voice 3			A	B	X	A.		

Our examples have shown that Eastern Europe possesses one of the richest traditions of folk music. Variety and regional diversity are tremendous, but if we had to divide the area into geographic subdivisions with some stylistic homogeneity, it would have to be into four groups: 1) the Western Slavs—Czechs, Slovaks, Poles—who tend to show the Western European characteristics and the influences of Western art music; 2) the Russians, Ukrainians, and Caucasians, whose main characteristic is the highly developed polyphony; 3) the Balkan peoples, with their small intervals and the strong influence of the Near East; and 4) the Hungarians and other Finno-Ugric peoples who, in spite of their isolation from each other, have retained some elements of their common heritage, such as the penta-

EXAMPLE 5-9. Lithuanian round in three parts, from pamphlet accompanying the recording *Lithuanian Folk Song in the United States* (New York: Folkways Records P 1009), p. 4-5.

tonic scale without half tones and the practice of transposing phrases as an essential part of song structure.

Bibliography and discography

The folk music of some of the Western nations in Eastern Europe is the field that has been so thoroughly studied by Béla Bartók and Zoltán Kodály, and their publications are to be recommended here although all of them cannot be mentioned. Bartók's *Slovenske l'udovne piesne* (Bratislava: Slovakian Academy of Sciences, 1959–) is a monumental collection of Slovak folk song which also shows his method of classifying the songs. Zoltán Kodály, *Folk Music of Hungary* (London: Barrie and Rockliff, 1960) is an important discussion. Bartók's *Melodien der rumänischen Colinde* (Vienna: Universal Edition, 1935) includes the melodies of hundreds of Rumanian Christmas carols.

Among the many good readings on Yugoslav folk music, we suggest Bartók and Albert B. Lord, *Serbo-Croatian Folk Songs* (New York: Columbia University Press, 1951); Albert B. Lord, "Yugoslav Epic Folk Poetry," *J-IFMC*, III (1951), 57-61; and George Herzog, "The Music of Yugoslav Heroic Epic Folk Poetry," *J-IFMC*, III (1951), 62-64. Two important discussions of Greek folk music are Solon Michaelides, *The Neohellenic Folk-Music* (Limassol, Cyprus: Nicosia, 1948) and Rodney Gallop, "Folksongs of Modern Greece," *Musical Quarterly*, XXI (1935), 89-98. A detailed discussion of one Balkan style is Boris Kremenliev, *Bulgarian-Macedonian Folk Music* (Berkeley: University of California Press, 1952). *Treasured Polish Songs with English Translations*, published by Polanie Club, selected by Josepha K. Contoski (Minneapolis: Polanie, 1953) is a collection for practical use, as is Rose Rubin and Michael Stillman, *A Russian Song Book* (New York: Random House, 1962). Polyphonic Russian songs are collected in A. Listopadov, *Pesni Donskikh Kazakov* (Moscow: Musgys, 1949–). Aspects of Caucasian folk music are discussed in Victor Belaiev, "Folk Music of Georgia," *Musical Quarterly*, XIX (1933), 417-33. The music of one special ethnic group in the USSR is presented in Bruno Nettl, *Cheremis Musical Styles* (Bloomington: Indiana University Press, 1960).

The following records give samplings of Eastern European folk music: *Czech, Slovak and Moravian Folk Songs*, Monitor MF 389; *Czech Songs and Dances*, Apon 2473; *Folk Music of Hungary*, collected under the auspices of Béla Bartók, Folkways P 1000; *Folk Music of Yugoslavia*, Folkways 4434; *Folk Music of Rumania*, collected by Béla Bartók, Folkways 419; *Folk Dances of Greece*, Folkways FE 4467; *Folk Music of Greece*, Folkways FE 4454; *Polish Folk Songs and Dances*, Folkways FP 848; and *Russian Folk Songs*, Vanguard VRS 9023, a recording performed by professional interpreters.

6

France, Italy, and the Iberian Peninsula

The area comprising France, Italy, Spain, and Portugal is distinguished by its particularly long and close association with art and church music. This is especially true of France and Italy, the nations which perhaps more consistently than any others have had a tradition of sophisticated music and of urban civilization since the Middle Ages. It has often been thought that these countries have little folk music except that which trickled down from the cities, and which we call *gesunkenes Kulturgut*. To be sure, there have been some successful attempts to trace the history of certain song and dance types back to the medieval troubadours and trouvères, and to the earliest known forms of instrumental music (such as the stantipes, which consists of a series of repeated musical lines with first and second endings, like that of the *branle* in Example 6-1). But recently, folklorists have also uncovered enclaves in which folk music seems to have developed with much less influence from the cities, and they have found interesting and unexpected styles.

Some aspects of French folk music

In France, the main areas preserving old traditions are in the South, near the Pyrenees, and Brittany. On the whole, the French folk songs have the same kinds of functions as those in England, Germany, and the Low Countries. Ballads are perhaps not so prominent, while lyrical love songs, humorous songs, and dance music are among the most numerous types.

A large number of dances—whether they were used in the peasant culture, in the towns, or at the courts we don't always know—are described already in sources dating from the Renaissance, notably in Thoinot Arbeau's *Orchésographie* (1589); and a number of these dances are still alive in folklore today. Notable among them is the *branle*, performed either as a round dance or by two lines of dancers facing each other, in moderately quick duple meter. Example 6-1 is

EXAMPLE 6-1. French instrumental piece, "Branle carré," played on hurdy-gurdy; melody only, transcribed by Bruno Nettl from the recording, *Folk Music of France* (New York: Folkways Record P414A), band 1.

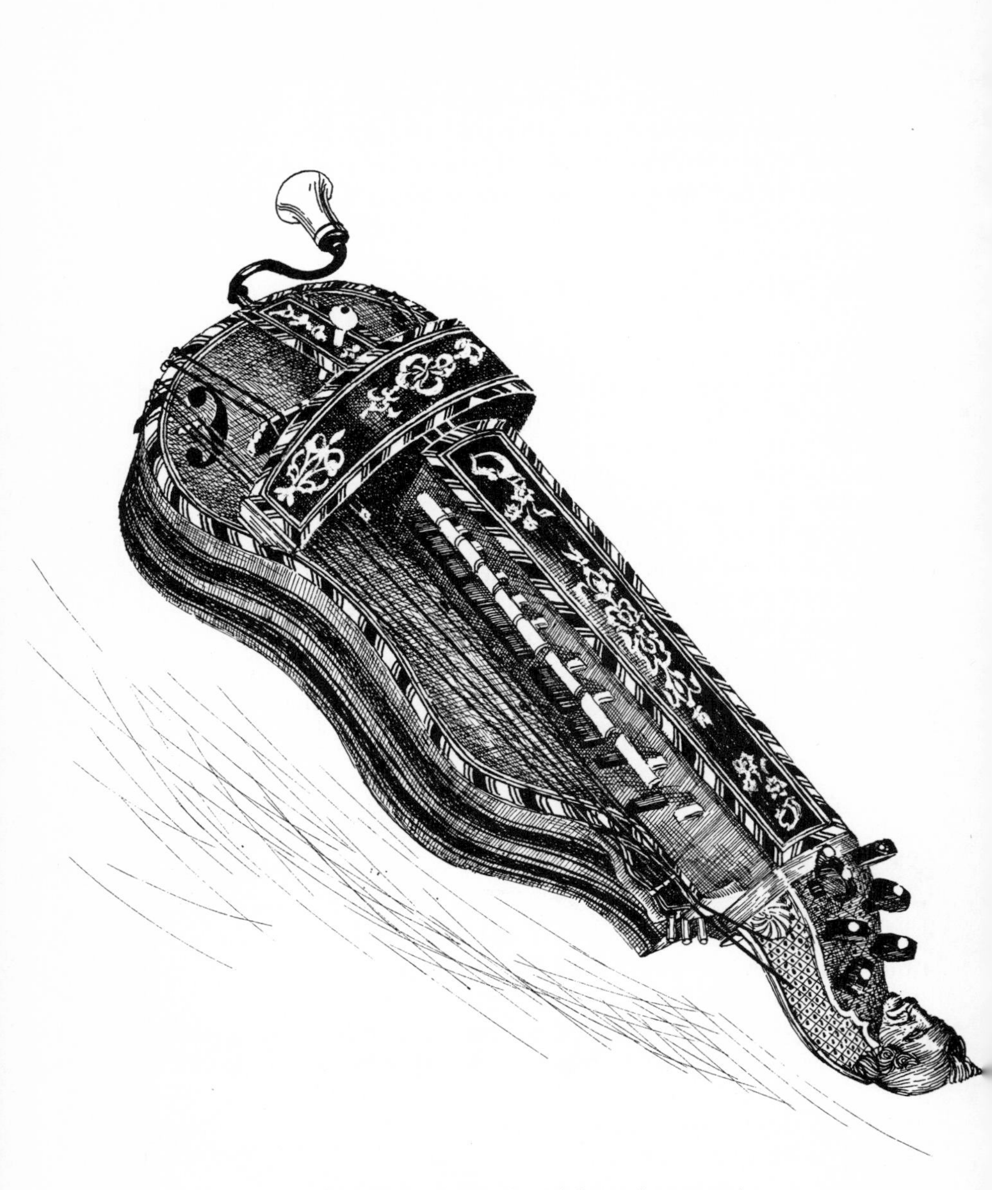

French hurdy-gurdy (eighteenth century).

an example performed on the hurdy-gurdy (French *vielle*, but not to be confused with an early type of viol also called by that name). The tune is heptatonic, using both F and F-sharp, and could be considered as being in major if it also made use of the note A. Its form is characteristic of many dance tunes in various parts of Europe (even the Cheremis near the Urals use it), repeating a phrase with first and second endings, then repeating the pair, and then going on to a contrasting phrase that is repeated in the same fashion. The instrument used gives this piece an especially interesting character. The hurdy-gurdy—not to be confused with the barrel organ known also by that name—is widespread in Western Europe and goes back at least to the ninth century, when it was known as *organistrum*. It has a number of strings, all but one of which are used as drones. The single melody string has mechanical stops which are activated by a keyboard. Sound is produced by a rosined wheel which touches all strings simultaneously and which is turned constantly so that the music consists of unbroken melodic line accompanied by drone; this gives the music a bagpipe-like effect.

The importance of melodies accompanied by drones is remarkable in European folk music, perhaps sufficiently so to make this one of the special characteristics of Europe. The drone is of great importance in Middle and Near Eastern music as well, however. A number of otherwise unrelated instruments seem fashioned especially for use as drones. Besides the hurdy-gurdy there is, of course, the bagpipe (which is common in France, known as *cornemuse*, and was evidently popular there for centuries, as is attested by the many pieces entitled entitled "Musette" in seventeenth- and eighteenth-century art music). The double flutes or clarinets of the Balkans, such as the Yugoslav *dvojnice*, use one pipe for melody, the other for drone. The dulcimer is frequently used in similar fashion. But even in the music of instruments that because of their structure are not especially suited to drones, the drone principle is often present. Thus, Anglo-American fiddle players often strike open strings in addition to the melody tones, producing a kind of interrupted drone effect. And the chordal accompaniment on instruments such as the banjo and the guitar frequently revolves around a single chord, which gives an effect related to the drone.

In spite of regional diversity and even though archaic styles of French music exist in isolated pockets, the predominant style of

French folk music shows the tremendous impact that art music through the centuries must have had. The typical tunes are isometric, they have major or (much less commonly) melodic minor tonality, they are monophonic or accompanied by chord or drones, and they move briskly in strophic forms. Singing is with relaxed voice and with little ornamentation. The fact that some of the French forms can be related, whether through the etymology of their names or through their structure, to some of the genres of music (such as the dances) of the Renaissance and Middle Ages should prove to us the close kind of contact extant between art and folk music. In the last three or four centuries, this relationship can again be shown in the diffusion of the quadrille and its relative, the square dance. This type of dance evidently originated in France some time before the eighteenth century and was a sort of transition between round and couple dances. It became a dance popular in the cities and at the courts, had a period of being stately and dignified, and then was again accelerated. In the nineteenth century it gradually declined as a dance of the city folk but found its way again into folk culture, eventually becoming the typical folk dance of the English-speaking world. Similarly, remnants of medieval forms of troubadour song seem to have found their way into contemporary folk culture. Thus, Carlos Vega[1] believes that he has found variants of medieval troubadour melodies from Provence in Argentine folk tradition. Accordingly, French folklore is one of the best examples of the occasional validity of the theory of *gesunkenes Kulturgut.*

Polyphonic Italian folk song

For several decades in the twentieth century it was widely believed that Italy had no folk music, that the country had been in the grip of musical sophisticates for so long that no folk heritage with its characteristic traits—oral tradition, communal re-creation, and the like—still remained. In the 1950's, however, through the collecting efforts of several scholars including Diego Carpitella and Alan Lomax, a great treasure of folksongs relatively uninfluenced by art music and exhibiting great variety of style and forms was uncovered.

[1] Carlos Vega, in a paper read at the First Inter-American Conference on Musicology, Washington, D.C., May, 1963.

Carpitella[2] believes that a rather sharp division exists between an ancient style, which is found largely in the lullabies, work songs, and funeral laments, and a modern style. The ancient style is characterized by the church modes and, occasionally, by scales with five and fewer tones. The later style (which evidently really did come about through the growth of art music) is characterized by the use of major and of harmonic and melodic minor scales. The ancient style is found mainly in those regions of Italy which have remained relatively isolated from modern developments in technology and economics, and which, even after 1950, had a noticeably lower standard of living than did the rest of the nation; these regions are South and Central Italy and the islands of Sicily and Sardinia.

Among the most interesting finds of the recent upsurge in ethnomusicological research in Italy is a rich tradition of polyphony. Among the simpler instances is Example 6-2, a kind of duet recitative. The beginning by a soloist who is joined by a second voice is typical of this style, though not found in this example (see Example 5-8 for a Ukrainian example of this feature which is found in many European countries and in Africa). In Example 6-2, the movement is largely in parallel thirds, which is a feature also common in Italian popular and light classical music. The moving apart of the voices from a unison, beginning with the seventh note, the parallel fifths in

EXAMPLE 6-2. Italian polyphonic folk song, from Alberto Favara, *Corpus di Musiche Siciliane* (Palermo: Accademia de Scienze, Lettere e Arti, 1957), vol. 1, p. 225.

the middle, and the ending on a unison remind us of examples of medieval *organum*.

A characteristic of some of the more complex Italian polyphony

[2] Diego Carpitella, "Folk Music: Italy," *Grove's Dictionary of Music and Musicians*, 5th edition (New York: St. Martin's Press, 1960), X, 137.

is the alternation of melodic movement among the voices. While one voice sings a bit of melody, the other one remains sustained; in the next phrase, the previously sustained voice becomes the carrier of the melody, and so on in alternation. The use of different kinds of rhythmic structure in each voice is also typical: one voice may carry the main tune, another may sing sustained notes supplying harmony, while a third may sing a rapid rhythmic figure on one tone, with meaningless syllables, perhaps imitating a drumbeat. Polyphonic singing is found in various kinds of Italian song—shepherds' songs, songs of dock workers and sailors. Some of the polyphony makes use of instruments as well as of singing; in such cases the singers are often accompanied, again, by instruments that can produce a drone—bagpipes, a small organ, or the *launeddas*, which is discussed below.

The influence of cultures outside Italy on Italian polyphony may explain some of the regional differences. The North of Italy, which is dominated by the more modern style of folk song and by singing in parallel thirds and sixths, has had close contact with the Alpine musical cultures with their love of triadic structures. The South has had less contact with Europe and has preserved older forms. Influences from Africa and the Near East can perhaps also be felt in the South. According to Carpitella,[3] a type of song sung in the tunny-fishery areas near North Africa is characterized by the kind of call-and-response patterns common also in African Negro music and found sometimes in North Africa as well. If he is correct in his belief that this song type actually came from Africa, he has come upon an interesting early example of the kind of influence that African music, in the last two centuries, has exercised so strongly on Western folk music, for it is precisely this call-and-response pattern which has been the cornerstone of the various Afro-American styles in folk and popular music.

Some other aspects of Italian folk music

The instruments most evident in Italian folk music are those which have been taken over from the cultivated tradition: violin, guitar, mandolin, clarinet, accordion. But there are also much older instruments, some of which seem to have remained relatively unchanged since classical times, in the more isolated parts of the nation.

[3] Carpitella, "Folk Music: Italy," p. 140.

There are various percussion instruments (clappers, rattles), conch trumpets, the Jew's harp, panpipes, simple bagpipes with up to three drone pipes, recorder-like plugged flutes, reed pipes, and ocarinas made of fired clay. One of the most intriguing is the *launeddas*, found mainly in Sardinia, which consists of three reed pipes. The longest and shortest of these are fastened together and held in the left hand (these are called *tumbu* and *mancosedda*, respectively); the middle-sized one, *mancosa*, is held in the right hand. The *launeddas* is used for polyphonic music of the drone type, similar to that played on the Yugoslav *dvojnice*. One of the problems faced by the player is the need to keep blowing without pausing for breath; it is solved by a technique of blowing air out of the mouth while inhaling with the nose. A boy learning to play the *launeddas* learns this technique, as have Mediterranean musicians since Egyptian antiquity, by practicing blowing through a straw into a pail of water. The teacher can see whether the pupil is succeeding by observing the bubbles in the water.

The close relationship between Italian folk and art music during the past few centuries is also illustrated by the sources of the words of some of the songs. In Central Italy, a type of song (or perhaps a sequence of songs) known as *maggio* is sung during May. Its words are frequently taken from the works of famous poets—Ariosto, Tasso, Dante, even Classical poets such as Virgil and Ovid. Its structure is evidently related to some of the earliest manifestations of opera around 1600. The form of the *maggi* consists of a choral or instrumental introduction, recitatives, and instrumental or choral interludes which recur, functioning rather like refrains or *ritornellos* (instrumental refrain-like pieces in early opera). In thematic content the various parts of a *maggio* are not necessarily related· the recitative may be in the modal style of ancient Italian folk music, the choral section may have some features found in the part-songs of Renaissance Italian art music, and the instrumental sections may be popular dances such as polkas or tarantellas.

Peculiarities of the Basque heritage

Legend has it that the Basques are the oldest people in Europe, but they seem to have retained little of their ancient heritage of folklore. On the contrary, they seem to have partaken of the traditions of Northern Spain and Southwestern France, and their culture is a repository of archaic forms of that region, both French and Spanish. For example, young Basque men have a custom, also found in other parts of Europe, of going from house to house on the last Saturday of January, wishing the inhabitants good health and a good life, and singing songs to them. Elsewhere, this may be done before Christmas and even at Easter, and the singers may be young boys and girls. Another custom shared by the Basques with some other areas of Europe is the singing of "rough music" around the house of people who have engaged in some presumably immoral act.[4] An adulterous couple, an old man who marries a young girl, or a wife who beats her husband may be visited by a group who use pots, pans, and cowbells as rhythmic accompaniment to improvised, insulting songs. In Germany and other countries, similar "music" is performed on a wedding night or on the night before a wedding.

We know very little about the ways in which European folk songs were composed, and about the techniques of composition in folk cultures. This applies to words as well as music, although we realize that some of the material is composed by sophisticated song writers and then passed into oral tradition. Among the Basques, improvisation is particularly important; it is even thought that most of the Basque folk songs originated on the spur of the moment. Evidently the Basque language (which is said to be so difficult that not even the devil can learn it) lends itself easily to improvisatory riming. Many of these improvised poems have a humorous or satirical character and deal with recent events of village interest, politics, and the church. Many are anticlerical in sentiment. Evidently the improvised text was sung to a traditional tune, and most Basque men participated in the practice of improvising words. A few of them gained preëminence, and some of their songs still carry their names after years and decades. This is one of the few examples in a folk culture of a composer's being recognized and associated with his own works years after he composed them. The most famous Basque improviser, or *kolaris*, was known as Etchahoun and was born in the valley of Soule in 1786.

Like a large proportion of the Spanish and French songs, Basque

[4] Rodney Gallop, "Basque Songs from Soule," *Musical Quarterly* XXII (1936), 461.

songs are frequently in 6/8 meter and make use of the church modes; the latter is true of the ballad in Example 6-3, which is Dorian.

But more complex meters, such as 5/8, are also common, as are songs without ascertainable metric structure. The most famous illustration of quintuple meter in Basque folk music is the *zortziko*, a

EXAMPLE 6-3. French singing game, "Yan petit," from Violet Alford, "Dance and Song in Two Pyrenean Valleys," *Musical Quarterly* XVII (1931), 253.

type of melody used mainly for dance tunes. The forms of Basque songs consist of from four to six phrases, interrelated in various ways. Lullabies frequently consist of varied repetitions of a single musical line (A^1 A^2 A^3 . . .), while love songs and dance songs have forms such as ABCC, ABCB, AABCD, AABB, and AABCDC.

Instrumental folk music among the Basques features a three-holed flute (*chirula*) and the *ttun-ttun*, an instrument similar to the dulcimer, but held in the arm, with six strings. The same player uses both instruments, accompanying the tunes of the *chirula* with a drone on the *ttun-ttun*. Instrumental music is used in dances and for "mascaradas," processions accompanied by dances performed at carnival time. Again, this custom is one found throughout Europe, but it is preserved in very elaborate form in the Basque country. Ceremonial dances are performed by certain stock characters—the hobby horse, which is surely a remnant of the tournaments of the Middle Ages, the fool, the sweeper, and the lord and the lady. Similar practices are found among the Negroes of Uruguay, where the *candombe,* interestingly enough, features a broom-maker analogous to our "sweeper" (see Chapter 9). There is a sword dance which, like those of France, Spain, and England, was probably originally a representation of the century-long struggle between Christians and Moors. There is also an acrobatic dance in which dancers leap and turn complicated steps around and over a tumbler of wine without upsetting it. The instrumental music is similar in style to the songs, but the song tunes themselves do not normally seem to be used by instrumentalists.

The Basques have also retained a form of the medieval mystery play, called *Pastorales.* These folk plays make use of interpolated songs which appear at particularly important points in the plot. The themes of the *Pastorales* are biblical or legendary and frequently hark back to the battles of Christians against Moors in the Iberian peninsula. No matter what the plot, the characters are divided into Moors or Turks dressed in red costumes, and Christians, in blue. The battles for national or cultural survival in Spain and France have evidently had just as great an impact on the development of folklore as have the struggles against the Turks in Yugoslavia, with its epic tradition, or as did the fights between Christian and Tartar in Russia.

Spain and Portugal

There is tremendous variety in the folk music of the Hispanic peninsula, each region having its own styles. There are the special types of music used by the Spanish gypsies, by the Basques, in the southern areas influenced by Arabic music, and in the Provencal section whose music owes much to that of France. Nevertheless, there is also considerable unity: few listeners would fail, after some experience, to recognize a Spanish folk melody. Of course, the many kinds of folk songs found in Spain have also spread to Latin America, where they form the basis of the main body of folklore, and a few of these are mentioned again in Chapter 10.

It is difficult to identify and separate those traits which make Spanish folk music sound "Spanish" (here we must include Portugal as a region of Spain). Triple meter abounds: slow triple meter, usually notated as 3/4, and quicker, compound meters such as 6/8 and 9/8 are very common. But songs in duple meter are also found, as are some in quintuple. There is also a good deal of recitative-like singing, without obvious metric structure, and with considerable ornamentation. Scales tend to be diatonic, and the tonality major, natural minor, or with the use of augmented and minor seconds, thus: . The forms of the songs are usually strophic, similar to those of Italy and France, but in many cases somewhat less regular as far as the relative length of the lines is concerned. There is a good deal of polyphonic singing, mainly in parallel thirds or sixths or with the accompaniment of a drone.

The influence of Arabic music on Spanish folk song seems to have been considerable, which is not surprising when we remember the centuries of Arab rule over the peninsula (the ninth through the fifteenth centuries). Specific tunes from the Arabic tradition do not seem to have remained in any large numbers, however. Possibly the scales with augmented seconds may have been introduced by the Arabs, or they may have developed as a result of the Arabic influence, since such intervals are a typical feature of much Arabic music. The great amount of ornamentation found in some of the melodies that have no metric structure may also ultimately be of Near Eastern origin, for singing of a related sort is found in some Arabic music of today. Example 6-4 is such a melody from Santander.

Perhaps a more important feature common to Spanish and Arabic music is the manner of singing, which is rather tense, nasal, and harsh-sounding. Ornaments of a modest sort are found in many songs; the mordent and the turn are particularly common. The tempo of Spanish songs may be either rapid, vigorous and downright driving, or slow and stately.

Among the many kinds of song in Spain and Portugal we should mention the *copla*, which is a short, lyrical type, usually with only

EXAMPLE 6-4. Spanish folk song, from Kurt Schindler, *Folk Music and Poetry of Spain and Portugal* (New York: Hispanic Institute in the United States, 1941), song no. 530.

one stanza. Ballads are also found in Spain; they deal, typically, with the heroism of the medieval warriors such as Charlemagne and El Cid, and their content has more in common with the epics of Eastern Europe than with the tragic ballads of Britain, impersonal as the latter usually are. The arrangement of a group of ballads around a hero is rather like the clustering of epic tales around a leader such as the Serbian Kraljevic Marko (Prince Marko), and it has something in common with the cycle of Robin Hood ballads, which were once sung throughout Great Britain. Some of the themes of Spanish balladry are of wide provenience, however; the same stories have been found, on occasion, in French and Scandinavian songs.

When one thinks of Spanish folk music one perhaps thinks automatically of dancing, and, of course, there are many Spanish folk dance types: the *jota*, the *gitana*, the *seguidillas*, the *bolero*, the *fandango*, the *murciana*, and others too numerous to mention. Each district has its own version of the dance types of national provenience. The *jota*, a combination of song and dance, is one of the most interesting. In rapid triple meter, it is danced by a couple—originally it was probably a dance of courtship—whose complicated footwork and difficult castanet rhythms are especially fascinating.

The *flamenco* tradition of Andalusia in Southern Spain is perhaps the most widely known aspect of Spanish folk music. It is not typically Spanish, for it is particularly the music of the Spanish gypsies, although it probably did not originate with them but was simply taken over by them. The gypsies, who inhabit many countries of Southern and Eastern Europe, have a tradition of entertaining and, evidently, a talent for emphasizing and exaggerating the most characteristic elements of the folk music in each country in which they live (in addition to continuing their native tradition). Thus, for example, the Russian gypsies have developed a style out of the Russian folk tradition, and the Spanish gypsies have fashioned the *flamenco* style out of elements already present in Spain.

A type of *flamenco* music is the *cante hondo*, which means "deep" or "profound song." The words are frequently tragic, sometimes verses of complaint against injustices. The range of these songs rarely exceeds a sixth, and the structure is not strophic but consists of irregular repetitions and alternations of two or more phrases with variations. The singing is highly ornamented and contains occasional microtones. It is often accompanied by the guitar, which performs simple repetitive chord sequences in rapid triple meter: .

The words of *flamenco* proper are usually erotic, and the dance is performed by a soloist or a couple, with the audience participating with encouraging shouts of *olé*.

The close relationship between Spain and the folk music of other continents—it received material from Africa which ultimately came from Asia, and in turn it was the agent of diffusion to the Americas—provides a good note for closing a discussion of European folk music. As European culture as a whole received much of its basic materials for forming a tradition of folk music from Asia (and possibly from Africa), it passed on this heritage to the Americas and to other colonized areas, from which it in turn was stimulated. Similarly, Spanish folk music has much in common with that of its European neighbors and something with that of the European Near East. But in spite of the many influences that each national tradition has received from the outside, each one has developed, through its own way of assimilating and combining these influences, a characteristic degree of uniqueness.

Bibliography and discography

An interesting collection of French folk song is Émile Barbillat and Laurian Touraine, *Chansons Populaires dans le Bas-Berri* (Paris: Gargaillou, 1930-1931, 5 vols.). The best discussion in English of French folk music is in the fifth edition of Grove's *Dictionary of Music and Musicians,* under "Folk Music" in the subdivision on France (by C. Marcel-Dubois). Rodney Gallop, "Basque Songs from Soule," *Musical Quarterly*, XXII (1936), 458-69, and Violet Alford, "Dance and Songs in Two Pyrenean Valleys," *Musical Quarterly*, XVII (1931), 248-58 are interesting readings on the area common to France and Spain. A large and comprehensive collection of Spanish and Portuguese music is Kurt Schindler, *Folk Music and Poetry of Spain and Portugal* (New York: Hispanic Institute, 1941). The best discussion, in English, of Italian folk music is in Grove's *Dictionary of Music and Musicians*, fifth edition, the supplement volume (1960)—not the section on Italian folk music in the body of the fifth edition. Alberto Favara, *Corpus di Musiche Popolari Siciliane* (Palermo: Accademia di scienze, lettere e arti, 1957, 2 vols.) is a comprehensive collection from Sicily. Discussion of one song type appears in Wolfgang Laade, "The Corsican Tribbiera, a Kind of Work Song," *Ethnomusicology*, VI (1962), 181-85.

For selections of French, Hispanic, and Italian folk music, the appropriate disks from the *Columbia World Library of Folk and Primitive Music* are especially useful. Also to be recommended are *Folk Music of France,* Folkways P 414; *Folk Music from Italy*, Folkways F 4220; *Songs and Dances of Spain*, Westminster WF 12001-5, with notes by Alan Lomax; *Flamenco Music of Andalusia*, Folkways 4437; and *Music of Portugal*, Folkways 4538 (2 disks).

7

African Music South of the Sahara

If you have heard a few recordings of African Negro music, you will probably have no difficulty in recognizing other pieces from this, one of the most interesting style groups in the realm of traditional music. There is indeed a great deal of homogeneity in the music of this vast area, but it has become clear that there are also differences among the regions and tribes.

We are considering the music of Africa south of the Sahara, only, in this volume. Perhaps we are not especially justified in splitting this continent into Northern and sub-Saharan areas, for the Negro cultures have evidently carried on a lively exchange of music with the lighter-skinned inhabitants of the northern part of Africa.

Moreover, there is a large area of borderline cultures that are related to both the Negro and the North African societies. But the area north and immediately east of the Sahara and the Sahara itself are inhabited by peoples whose culture and music have been under the influence of Islamic culture for centuries. Their music sounds similar to Arabic music, and it is better discussed in the volume on Asian music in this series. The area South of the Sahara, on the other hand, strange as it may sound to those of us used to hearing only European music, seems to have some very general stylistic similarities with the latter. But the most obvious reason for including African Negro music in this volume is its close relationship to the music of Negro groups in the Americas.

The part of Africa discussed here—and, for the sake of brevity, we will call it simply "Africa" from now on—is composed of (or was, before parts of it became thoroughly Westernized) four culture areas, each of which has a good deal of homogeneity, and each of which contrasts in some rather specific ways with its neighbors. The western part of the very tip of Southern Africa is called the Khoi-San area, and it is inhabited by the Bushmen and Hottentots. The Bushmen are a somewhat different group, racially, from Negroes, shorter and lighter skinned; the Hottentots are evidently the result of a racial mixture between Bushmen and Negroes. The Khoi-San area has a simple culture dependent mainly on nomadic gathering of food.

The eastern part of our Africa, from Ethiopia southward, is called the Eastern Cattle Area. Its cultures are complex and revolve about cattle, which is the chief item of economic goods and the symbol of wealth. Some of the tribes are warlike; some, such as the Masai and Watusi, are very tall and rule over neighboring tribes of smaller stature.

The southern coast of the western extension of the continent, which includes Ghana, Nigeria, Ivory Coast, and Liberia, is known as the Guinea Coast. This area lacks cattle and is characterized by elaborate political organization which, before the imposition of European rule, gave rise to powerful kingdoms. Carved masks of great beauty are also typical here. The Congo area, north of the Khoi-San area and centered in the Congo republics, has to some extent a combination of Eastern Cattle and Guinea Coast traits. It includes a number of Pygmy and Negrito tribes who live in relative isolation in the jungle. The Congo area probably has the most highly developed visual art tradition in Africa.

The uses of music in Africa

In Africa, music has many uses. It performs the function of accompanying all sorts of activities, but there is also music for entertainment. Some of the general characteristics usually given for music in nonliterate societies do not appear strongly in Africa. For example, the idea that participation in music in a primitive society is quite general and that all persons participate equally cannot be accepted. In contrast to many tribes elsewhere, there are professional musicians who actually make their living from music, or who are regarded as trained specialists. There are so many instruments that it would be ridiculous to think that all members of a tribe could perform on all of them and know all of the tribe's music. But it cannot be denied that Africans, on the whole, do participate in musical life much more —and more actively, singing, playing, composing, dancing—than do members of Western civilization.

Obviously, also, Africans think about music a good deal. For example, some tribes recognize many different types of songs and have elaborate terms for them. Thus, according to Merriam,[1] the Bahutu of Ruanda have at least twenty-four different types of social songs, including "those played by professional musicians for entertainment, songs for beer drinking, war homage to a chief, hunting, harvesting, and general work; songs sung at the birth of a child or to admonish erring members of the society, to recount a successful elephant hunt, to deride Europeans; songs of death, vulgar songs, and others." These categories are separate from the other large group of ceremonial or religious songs. Some of these types are again subdivided by the Bahutu, who, for example, distinguish among different kinds of songs associated with canoes: Different songs are used when paddling against a strong current, when paddling with the current, and so forth.

The Watusi, also of Ruanda, whose lives center about their cattle, have many song types involving cattle: "songs in praise of cows,

[1] Alan P. Merriam, "African Music" in *Continuity and Change in African Cultures,* ed. William Bascom and Melville J. Herskovits (Chicago: University of Chicago Press, 1959), p. 50.

songs to indicate the importance of having cows, songs for taking cattle home in the evening . . . for drawing water for the cattle,"[2] and the like. There are special children's cattle songs, songs to praise the royal cattle, and songs that recount historical events in which cattle have played a part. There are two points to be remembered here: This classification of songs is one developed by the Africans themselves; and the music is a part of those activities which are most fundamental in the culture. In this sense, perhaps, music in African life can be said to have a greater or more important role than it does in Western civilization.

It would be useless to attempt to catalogue all the uses of music in African Negro music. In many ways they parallel those of European folk music: Religious and ceremonial music is an ever-present category whose importance evidently increases as we move from complex to simpler cultures. The large amount of music for entertainment, such as the playing of xylophones at markets, is remarkable. Social songs, such as those mentioned above, are a larger category here than in most folk and nonliterate societies. The use of music for political purposes of various sorts should be noted. Evidently in some of the African tribes it is easier to indicate discontent with employers or with the government if the discontent is sung than if it is spoken. We therefore find many songs expressing criticism of authority, but also songs composed especially to praise chiefs and wealthy men. Songs are used also to spread current events of interest and gossip, and to perpetuate knowledge of these events, much in the way that broadside ballads functioned as newspapers in eighteenth-century England and America. Work songs—songs not only dealing with labor but also accompanying rhythmic work by groups and making it easier—are prominent in Africa. In the Western Congo, song-like passages appear in the litigations of clans and individuals who may argue about ownership of territory, wives, or honorific titles.

Music and tone languages

In addition to music in the proper sense of the word, the use of musical sounds for signaling purposes is common in Africa. The

[2] Merriam, "African Music," p. 53.

relaying of drum signals over a long distance is legendary; horns are also used for this purpose, and, for more conversational ends over short distances, the same principles may be applied to xylophones. In some tribes, signaling takes on the character of Morse code, that is, arbitrary signals are used to indicate words or concepts. More frequently, however, the system of signaling is tied to the pitch structure of the language. The languages spoken in Negro Africa belong mainly to three families: Khoi-San, characterized by the famous clicks, which is spoken by the Bushmen and Hottentots; Niger-Congo (including the Bantu group), which occupies most of the area through the Congo region and the Guinea Coast, and which is a closely knit group of languages clearly related to each other; and Sudanic, which is spoken in the northeastern region of Negro Africa, and which consists of languages whose common origin is surmised rather than concretely proved. Most of the Bantu and many of the Sudanic languages are tone languages; that is, the relative pitch at which a syllable is spoken is relevant to the meaning of the word. Thus, in Jabo, a language spoken in Liberia, there are four "tones"; that is, four different relative pitch levels of speech are distinguished for purposes of meaning, and we can number these from 1 to 4, highest to lowest. In Jabo,[3] the word *ba* may mean four different things, depending on the pitch. *Ba*(1) means namesake, *ba*(2) means "to be broad," *ba*(3) means "tail," and *ba*(4) is a particle expressing command. In signaling, the pitches of the words—or rather their internal relationship, for of course the language tones are not fixed pitches but can be understood only in terms of the pitch of the surrounding syllables and of their place within the speaker's voice range—are transferred to the drum. Jabo signaling is done with two drums, one large, the other smaller, made of hollowed logs with slits. They are not true drums, of course, but idiophones. The pitch on each drum is varied according to the place at which it is struck. And, interestingly, the two lower tones of the language are combined into one tone on the large drum. The fact that many words or sentences could have the same sequence of tones, and that in the drum language tones 3 and 4 are indistinguishable, would seem to make deciphering of messages difficult. Only a few men are qualified to signal, and only certain things should be said in signal

[3] George Herzog, "Speech-Melody and Primitive Music," *Musical Quarterly* XX (1934), 453.

language. Understanding must come from knowledge of the kinds of things likely to be signaled, and evidently the Jabo restrict themselves to expressing thoughts such as "our neighbors are on the warpath," or, more appropriately in this period of acculturation, "Hide! The tax collector approaches!"

Just what happens when words in a tone language are set to music for the purpose of creating song? Does the melody slavishly follow the pitch movement of the words? Or is there free melodic movement which violates and to some extent obscures the meaning of the words by ignoring the linguistic tones? Not too much is known about this intricate relationship between music and speech, but it is obvious that no simple rule describes it. And it may well be that each tribal culture has evolved its own accommodation between language and music in song. It is evident, however, that melody does not slavishly follow speech, but that the tones of the words do have an influence on shaping the melody. In Nigeria, the Ibo, according to one kind of analysis, use two tones, high and low. If it were possible to formulate a rule for Ibo according to a small sampling of songs, we would have to say that the musical pitch sometimes moves up and down in the same direction as the pitch in speech; that it sometimes remains the same while the speech tones change; but that pitch movement in the music is never contrary to that of the language.

On the other hand, an example from the Chewa in Central East Africa, where the language also has two tones (marked in Example 7-1 by acute and grave accents, respectively), indicates very close

EXAMPLE 7-1. Chewa song, from George Herzog, "Speech-melody and Primitive Music," *Musical Quarterly* XX (1934), 457.

correspondence. These examples are intended only to show some of the kinds of things that may be found; they should not be used to draw conclusions regarding the way tone languages are set to music throughout Africa.

Another example of the close relationship among music, language, and other activities appears in some of the xylophone music of the Jabo in Liberia. According to Herzog, a form of evening entertainment is the repeated playing of short phrases on large xylophones which consist of big slabs laid across banana tree trunks.[4] These phrases are ordinary music to most listeners, but to a few who have inside knowledge they are musical versions of the tone patterns of sentences commenting on current events or mocking a member of the tribe. The person being mocked may not realize it, and the audience may burst into laughter when a piece that makes fun of an oblivious bystander is played. Sometimes this music is performed by two players sitting on opposite sides of the xylophone. They may perform a single melody together, they may play a canon, or they may repeat a tiny contrapuntal piece based on the speech tones of two sentences or phrases.

General characteristics of African forms

The most striking thing about the forms of African music is their dependence on short units, and in many cases on antiphonal or responsorial techniques. Most African compositions do not have units as long as the stanzas of typical European folk songs. They consist of short phrases that are repeated systematically, or alternated, or on which are based longer melodies of a "*Fortspinnung*" type (i.e., no unit is repeated exactly), in which a motif will reappear in different forms. Typical of the brevity of the phrases is Example 7-1, which in actual performance was probably repeated about fifteen times.

In instrumental music, short forms of this type are also found distributed over a large part of Africa. Example 7-2, recorded in Johannesburg and performed on the musical bow, consists of a systematic repetition of a rhythmic phrase that uses only two fundamental pitches. The musical bow, presumably the oldest of string instruments, is shaped like a hunting bow and produces only a very soft sound unless a resonator such as a gourd or a box is attached. The resonator may bring out overtones. In many cases, the player uses his mouth as the resonator; then, by changing the shape of his

[4] George Herzog, "Canon in West African Xylophone Melodies," *Journal of the American Musicological Society* II (1949), 196-97.

mouth, he can vary the overtones brought out. The upper voice in Example 7-2 is produced by overtones, and it, of course, is varied; but the piece consists of the manifold repetitions of this phrase.

EXAMPLE 7-2. South African musical bow melody, from Charles M. Camp and Bruno Nettl, "The Musical Bow in Southern Africa," *Anthropos* L (1955), 75.

Solo performance is common enough in Africa, but the most characteristic African music is performed by groups and gives occasion to the use of alternating performance techniques of various kinds. We say "characteristic" because this kind of performance is more developed in Africa than elsewhere, and because it is this element which, more perhaps than any other, has been retained in the Negro cultures of the New World. The simplest of these alternating techniques is responsorial singing, the alternation between a leader and a group which is sometimes also called the "call-and-response" technique. Example 7-3, from the Republic of the Congo (Brazzaville), shows what may frequently happen in such a form. Drums and an iron bell provide a constant rhythmic background whose general outline and meter remain the same, but whose accent patterns and specific note values vary somewhat. A female soloist sings a two-measure phrase alternating with a two-measure monophonic phrase sung by a group of women. The two phrases are different in content, but are similar at the cadence.

Improvisation is an important feature in some African styles. Evidently there is some real improvisation: that is, the creation of music without the use of pre-existing models as the basis. But this seems to be rare. More common is improvisation in the form of varying a tune as it is being performed. The forms consisting of short phrases that are repeated many times lend themselves especially well to this kind of improvisation, since it is possible for a singer to begin with the standard version of a tune and then to improvise variations that depart increasingly from the standard. This is what happens in the successive repetitions of the soloist's phrase in Example 7-3. The members of the chorus also improvise variations, but they do not depart as much from the original.

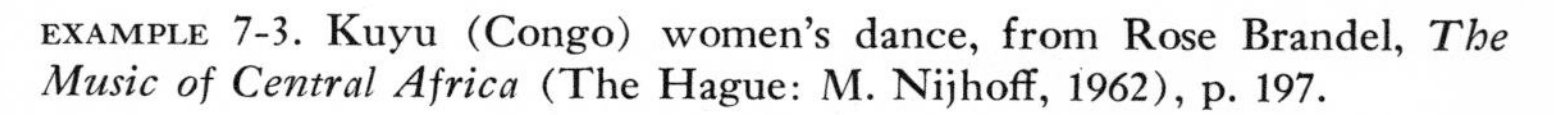
EXAMPLE 7-3. Kuyu (Congo) women's dance, from Rose Brandel, *The Music of Central Africa* (The Hague: M. Nijhoff, 1962), p. 197.

A further result of improvisation, presumably, is the creation of polyphonic forms. One of the characteristics of African music is harmony and polyphony, which are discussed below. Here it is relevant to point out that improvisation in choral and ensemble performance adds to the number of pitches heard at one time. Thus the fact that improvisation and variation is encouraged in some African cultures seems to have influenced the degree to which polyphony is accepted. Actually, variation by improvisation seems to be considered the mark of good musicianship in some African cultures. We should mention also a feature found in some African music that involves both form and polyphony, namely the tendency—in some pieces—for a number of apparently unrelated things to be going on at the same time. Some of this is due to the development of complex rhythmic polyphony, the simultaneous presentation of several meters which seem, to the Western listener, to have little in common. It is hard to say whether the African listener feels all of these rhythms to be part of one over-all rhythmic structure (as a Westerner can conceive all of the voices in a Bach fugue to be independent yet united), or whether the African can conceive of music as consisting of the simultaneous presentation of unrelated phenomena. At any rate, it is possible, in such a piece, to have phrases and other units of varying lengths appearing in different voices or instruments.

The forms of the songs and pieces, then, are usually short; but repetition may cause a performance of one piece to take many minutes and possibly even hours. The amount of repetition is usually determined by the time required by the activity that the music accompanies. And it is not uncommon, in a ceremony, to find musicians who have been performing one piece making an abrupt switch to the next musical item because the ceremonial activity has suddenly changed. Composite forms, consisting of series of pieces, are particularly common in ceremonial situations, where a large group of pieces, which may take a whole day or longer, must be performed in correct order to accompany ritual.

Melody

So far as the melodic elements of music are concerned, African music seems generally rather easily intelligible to the Western listener; it does not really have the exotic sound that some Oriental and some American Indian music has at first hearing. The conclusion we may tentatively draw from this fact is that African music, on the whole, fits more or less into the diatonic scheme that is also the basis of most Western art and folk music.

There have been attempts to identify a truly "African" scale. Ballanta-Taylor, an early West African scholar, believed that the basic scale of West African music has 16 tones per octave. Statements regarding the importance of pentatonic scales in Africa have been made. But the consensus of scholars is that there is no single system, that exact measurements of intervals would produce—at least in vocal music—a clustering about the intervals found also in diatonic scales, and that in many ways the kind of melodic structure in Africa corresponds to that of European folk music. As in Europe, we find songs with few tones—ditonic and tritonic scales—in Africa. There are pentatonic tunes with minor thirds and major seconds, and there are pentachordal ones as well. There are heptatonic songs, and there are occasional chromatic pieces. There are, moreover, intervals that do not fit into the diatonic scheme, such as neutral thirds (these are found also in Europe). There is, finally, a reported tendency in the heptatonic songs to use the intervals of minor third and minor seventh above the tonic. The interest in this feature stems from our desire to explain certain phenomena of jazz (the lowered seventh is a "blue note"), but it seems doubtful that these intervals constitute a special feature common to all African music. The fact that glides and ornaments are common in some African singing techniques also adds to the difficulty of defining a specific scale structure. Thus we must content ourselves with the generalization that African scales are varied but that as a group they seem to be closely related to those of Europe.

Types of melodic movement also exhibit great variety. In one area, Central Africa, we find the following kinds described by Brandel:[5] melodies clustering around a nucleus of one or two tones; melodies based on the perfect fourth, and descending directly from one tone to another a fourth below it, or making use also of the intervening tones; melodies built on the tones of the triad, and others using a whole string of thirds with only occasional use of intervening tones; melodies built on the triad with an added sixth (); melodies with the augmented fourth predominating, sometimes made up of three major seconds in a row (); and melodies with the

[5] Rose Brandel, *The Music of Central Africa* (The Hague: Martinus Nijhoff, 1961).

range of an octave or more, in which the lowest tone and its upper octave are the most important.

The melodic contours also have various types. Rather large ranges do seem to be characteristic of Africa. Europe has many songs with a range of less than a fifth, and relatively few (except for what appears to be recent material) having a range much larger than an octave. In African Negro music the number of pieces with a large range seems to be somewhat greater. Melodies move predominantly in three ways: 1) in a mildly undulating fashion, beginning on a low tone, rising gradually to a somewhat higher level, and returning to the low tone; 2) beginning on a high tone and descending; and 3) in what we may call a pendulum-like movement, swinging rapidly back and forth between high and low tones. Example 7-4 illustrates this pendulum-like movement, as well as the melodies made up largely of strings of thirds, discussed above.

EXAMPLE 7-4. Batwa Pygmy song (Ruanda), from Rose Brandel, *The Music of Central Africa* (The Hague: M. Nijhoff, 1962), p. 70.

In instrumental music, of course, melodic movement is more specialized, for each instrument makes possible or convenient certain kinds of movement, range, and interval. Thus, melodies played on the musical bow have a small range and use a melodic type clustering about one or two notes that are close together; horn music is likely to use larger intervals, while pendulum-like melody is more easily suited to the xylophone. We should also mention in this connection the great variety of tone colors achieved by the human voice. Yodeling, growling, raucous tones, and tense as well as relaxed singing are found. The imitation of animal cries and sounds of nature are a part of vocal music in Africa.

Rhythm

The feature of African music that has been most widely discussed is rhythm, and evidently it has indeed been more highly developed in Africa than have some other features or elements of music (such as melody and form). To some extent we may say that African rhythm is also more highly developed than the rhythm of other cultures. The latter statement must be made with caution, for certainly it would be possible for a composer of Western music to put together a piece with a rhythmic structure much more complex than that of any African piece. He could do this—especially with the techniques of electronic music. But the level at which African music seems to be rhythmically more developed is that of listener and performer perception. It is doubtful whether a Western listener could, without special training, perceive and reproduce the most complex structures in Western music, especially without a score, simply from sound. With training he might, of course, learn to match the performance and perception of African musicians. But this sort of training is not present in our culture, while it is—though not always formally—a part of African Negro musical training, for both the listener and the performer.

The rhythm of African music must be approached from two views. First, we are interested in the rhythmic structure (and its complexity) in a single melodic line. Here the rhythm and meter are usually not too difficult to understand. Metric structure with regular beats is common if not universal. Once beats are established it is possible to identify that widely discussed element, syncopation, which results from the regular articulation of notes at points other than the beginnings of beats. A distinctive feature of West African music that seems to have been carried over in Negro music of the New World is the ability of musicians to keep the same tempo for minutes and hours. Waterman refers to this ability (which no doubt is learned, not inherited) as the "metronome sense." We will never know, of course, whether such strict adherence to tempo has ever been practiced in Western music. Certainly in Western cultivated music in the twentieth century it is not found, something one can easily prove by playing a symphony recording and keeping time with a metronome. The rigid adherence to tempo may have made possible the considerable variety of rhythmic motifs and patterns in African music, for the musician who has a steady beat in his mind, and who does not deviate from it, can perhaps more easily elaborate the details of the rhythm. The compelling nature of rhythm is recognized in West African terminology, where the term "hot," applied to rhythmic drumming, evidently originated.[6] "Hot" rhythm in West Africa is particularly important in ceremonial music, and the more exciting the rhythm, the "hotter" the music is said to be.

The more spectacular rhythmic complexity of African Negro music appears, however, in the rhythmic polyphony, the superimposition of several rhythmic structures. Its most obvious manifestation is found in drumming, but of course it is also present in the combination of several voices or—more frequently—of instruments with voices. There is a great deal of drumming, but in other ways, also, the music seems to be dominated by a percussive quality. Individual tones in singing are attacked strongly, without a semblance of *legato*. There are few instruments on which one can slur notes together, and generally the music is vigorously accented. Thus the importance of drumming can perhaps be traced to the need for strong rhythmic articulation.

The perception of various simultaneous meters seems to be widespread among Africans. Rhythmic polyphony of a rather complex type can be performed by a single person who may sing in one meter and drum in another. The superimposition of duple and triple meters, called hemiola rhythm, is evidently a basic ingredient of much West and Central African rhythmic polyphony.

In music using three or more drums, the rhythmic polyphony is developed to its most complex level. While such music can be mechanically notated in a single meter, the various drummers are actually performing with independent metrical schemes; one drum may use duple, one triple, a third quintuple meter. Moreover, if the several drums or other instruments use the same basic metric scheme (such as 3/8), the beginning of the unit or measure may not come at the same time in all of the drums; thus we may have the following combination: 3/8, 5/8, 7/8, as in Example 7-5, which is a sample of Yoruba drumming with the pitch variations on the individual drum omitted.

The melodic element in drumming, as illustrated by the "royal drums" of the Watusi, which accompany the supreme chief whenever he emerges from his tent, is also important; drums used together always contrast in size and thus in pitch, and it is possible to

[6] Richard A. Waterman, " 'Hot' Rhythm in Negro Music," *Journal of the American Musicological Society* I (1948), 25f.

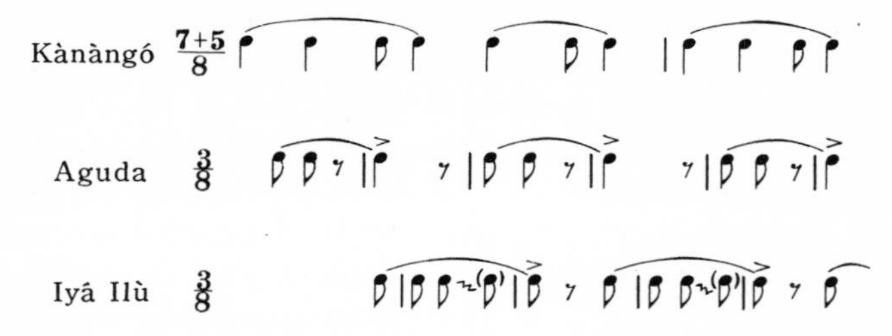

EXAMPLE 7-5. Yoruba drumming in honor of Ogun (god of war). The top part is the smallest and highest drum, the lowest part, the largest and lowest drum. From Anthony King, "Employment of the 'standard pattern' in Yoruba Music," *African Music II*, no. 3 (1960), 53.

follow each drum individually. In music using several melodic instruments, or voices and instruments, the structure of the rhythm is as complex as it is in the drumming, and the various voices often perform in different meters. To what extent the performers are listening to each other cannot always be ascertained, and to what degree a listener perceives the total rhythmic structure is also unknown.

Polyphony

Closely related to the rhythmic polyphony and to the question of perception of a group of individual rhythmic lines as a unit is the field of polyphony at large, and the question whether in Africa several voices are perceived independently or as a single vertical harmonic structure.

Whether it is polyphony or really harmony, it is very well developed in African Negro music. And it appears in many media. There is choral singing, usually in the responsory form. There is instrumental music of an orchestral nature, with a number of instruments of the same type playing together. And there is something similar to chamber music—instruments of different types playing together, alone or along with singing. Drumming and other percussion may of course act as accompaniment. Finally, there is also the concept of accompanying singing. There is polyphony of many types, and it seems to be present throughout the African Negro area, although it is concentrated in the Eastern cattle area and the Congo or Central Africa.

The fact that many kinds of polyphony are present in Africa—and that this also seems to be the case elsewhere in the world where polyphony is found—strengthens our belief that polyphony is a unified concept. When a culture discovers or learns to perform polyphony it seems to learn several different kinds. There are cultures with no polyphony at all, but there are few, if any, that use, say, only parallel fifths but nothing else.

Most African polyphony belongs to two types: 1) that in which all of the voices use the same melodic material, or 2) that which comes about through the peculiarities of the instruments. In the former category we find, of course, parallelism. There are parallel thirds, fourths, fifths, and occasionally sixths, but other intervals seem to be rare. In the case of parallel thirds, alternation between major and minor thirds is usual and is made necessary by the diatonic seven-tone scales which, as we have said, are common in Africa. Parallel fourths and fifths seem to be more common in East Africa, while thirds and sixths seem to dominate in the Congo and Guinea Coast areas. Parallelism is rarely completely exact, for the tendency to improvise seems to militate against slavish following of one voice by another. Example 7-6 illustrates parallelism among the Thonga of South Africa. A chorus of men and women is led by a female soloist and accompanied by a musical bow, which also plays interludes between the stanzas.

The player of the musical bow, which is evidently limited to the tones D, E, and F, plays the melody along with the soloist and with the second part of the chorus, but switches to an approximation of the highest part of the chorus when his range requires it.

African music also possesses rounds, which often seem to have come about through antiphonal or responsorial singing. If leader and chorus use the same tune, the chorus may become overanxious and fail to wait for the leader to finish his turn; thus a round of sorts is born. The fact that many African rounds do have the entrance of the second voice near the end of the first voice's rendition of a tune points to this manner of origin; so also does the fact that most known African rounds have only two voices. Also resulting from the antiphonal technique is the kind of polyphony in which one voice sustains a tone, perhaps the final tone of its phrase, while the other voice performs a more rapidly moving melody, at the end of which it, in turn, holds a long note while the first voice performs its moving part.

EXAMPLE 7-6. South African choral song with musical bow, from Charles M. Camp and Bruno Nettl, "The Musical Bow in Southern Africa," *Anthropos* L (1955), 80.

This gives rise to a sort of drone relationship between the voices.

There is also a relationship between the voices that could be called real counterpoint, but this seems to appear most frequently in instrumental music, where the structure of the instrument may in itself be conducive to certain melodic patterns and devices. Thus the accompaniment of singers on a harp, a xylophone, or a *mbira* (see page 138) may have nothing to do melodically with the tune of the singers. In the case of accompaniment, an "ostinato" relationship between voices and instruments is frequent. A short bit, perhaps a two-measure phrase, is repeated (with variations) by the instruments, while the singer or singers perform a longer melody which, however, is also repeated with improvised variations. This sort of structure is similar, of course, to that of much Western music, especially of popular or folk provenience; and Africans in the cities, who have come under the influence of Western popular music, have composed songs in which the African sort of accompaniment, by an ostinato figure, with a very short stanza by the singer, is used. We will have occasion to discuss the results of combining Western and African elements in the New World; but here is an example of the same sort of thing in modern Africa. In both places, those features in African music which are highly developed but which have a similar feature in its European counterpart seem to be preserved in the acculturated music of the Negroes.

Instruments

One of the characteristics of Negro Africa is its enormous variety of musical instruments. Far from being a land of drums, as it is pictured by some early sources, it is an area in which instruments and instrumental music play a role equal to that of the voice and vocal music. There is in all areas a great deal of music for solo instruments, and there are instrumental ensemble groups consisting of unrelated instruments, or of several instruments of the same type. Also, accompanied singing is widespread.

The importance of rhythm in African music can be seen in the percussive quality of much of the instrumental sound. Percussion instruments—drums, rattles, and melodic percussion instruments such as the xylophone—occupy a major role. Among the wind instruments, those in which each pipe performs only one note (panpipes or hocket-type performance on flutes or horns) are important. Among string instruments, those that are plucked are more prominent than the bowed ones. The percussive nature of much of the instrumental sound as well as the absence of the possibility of *legato* in the playing of most of the instruments are probably caused by the desire for strong rhythmic articulation.

It is impossible to describe or even to name all African instruments; but some of the most important ones are discussed briefly in the next few paragraphs. Among the idiophones (instruments whose bodies vibrate in order to produce sound), the xylophone is one of

East African xylophone with gourd resonators.

the most widespread. Consisting of anywhere from seven to twenty-five slabs of wood, it varies greatly in size. The largest ones lie on the ground supported by small tree trunks; the smallest hang around the player's neck. Xylophones are frequently built (in Central Africa) with calabashes, gourds, or other hollow bodies attached to the slabs in order to add to the resonance. They are frequently played in groups; in parts of Central Africa, three players will entertain at a market together. In the Eastern part of Southern Africa, among the Chopi, orchestras of six and more xylophones of various sizes are used. This point is of great interest, since there is some evidence for the belief that xylophones were brought to Africa from Indonesia, perhaps a thousand years ago. The people of Madagascar speak Malayo-Polynesian languages which must have originated near Indonesia. And the Indonesians have for centuries had a very complex musical culture with instruments, made of metal, of the xylophone type. It seems possible that the xylophone was brought to Africa, or that the musical culture of Indonesia influenced the particular direction in which xylophones and xylophone playing developed in Africa. Xylophones of the simplest type—one or two slabs of wood which are struck—are found throughout the world, including indigenous Latin America; this has evidently given rise to an erroneous belief that the xylophone (or rather, its form with resonators, the marimba) came from Central America and was brought thence to Africa.

An instrument that apparently originated in Africa, and which is related to the xylophone, is the *sansa* or *mbira*, which is sometimes also called the "thumb piano" or "kaffir harp." Its provenience is largely East and Central Africa, and except for some Negro cultures in the Americas, it is not found outside Africa. It consists of a small board or wooden box on which is nailed a bridge. Tied to this bridge are a number of "keys," made usually of iron pieces pounded flat, but occasionally of reeds. These are gently plucked by the thumb or the fingers to produce a soft, tinkling sound. The number of keys varies from eight to about thirty. Frequently a calabash resonator is attached to the instrument, and sometimes beads, which produce a rattling percussive accompaniment, are also attached. The *sansa* is played as a solo instrument, or in groups. It is frequently used to accompany singing, and in some African music of recent origin it is used to play an ostinato accompaniment not too different from the

Sansa or mbira.

piano accompaniments of certain Western popular songs. The tuning of both xylophone and *sansa* varies greatly. The keys of the *sansa* may be tuned by moving them forward or backward in relationship to the bridge, or by adding some pitch to them in order to increase their weight.

Other idiophones include rattles, bells, and the misnamed log drums. There are many types of rattles—pebbles enclosed in small woven containers (West Africa) and in antelope ears (the Hottentots); rattles made of fruits, nuts, reeds, or cocoons strung together (South Africa); and so on. Sometimes they are tied to the ankles of dancers. One characteristic of these idiophones is the importance evidently placed on distinctions in pitch. Rattles and bells (there are both metal and wooden bells) often appear in pairs, with one smaller than the other so that two pitches can be distinguished. This is also characteristic in the playing of the log drum idiophone, a hollowed log with one or two slits, which is most frequently used for signaling. Thus, while the rhythmic element seems to be pronounced in the melodic aspects of music and its instruments, we may also say that the melodic aspects of music are developed in that music and those instruments whose main function is rhythm.

There are several types of true drums, that is, drums with skin heads. The most common kinds have one head and are relatively tall; they are usually closed at the bottom. Two-headed drums and drums with an open end are also found. The drums are beaten with sticks, or with the hands, or both. Hand beating is characteristic, however, and the complex rhythms are often the results of intricate manipulation and alternation of fingers, thumb, and heel of the hand. Techniques somewhat similar to those of Africa are found in India, and there is a possibility that the rhythmic intricacies of India and Africa have a common origin. Typically drums are played in groups of three or more. They may stand on the ground, hang from a strap around the player's shoulder, be held in the player's arm or between his legs, or be sat upon when they are played.

The types of drums and of drumming may be intimately associated with different activities. Among the Yoruba of Nigeria, different types of drums are used for the various cults associated with the numerous gods in the Yoruba pantheon. For example, the *igbin* drums are upright drums with a single head, open-ended, with small wooden legs; *dundun* are kettle-drums with the skin stretched across a small bowl; *bata* drums are long truncated cones with two heads, one head being appreciably smaller than the other and producing a higher pitch. And there are several other types among the Yoruba. Each type is used for one or several deities, and each deity has its distinctive rhythms, a practice carried over into parts of the Americas such as Haiti. Thus, as Bascom notes,[7] the *igbin* drums are sacred to *Orishanla* ("the great deity") and are played by members of his cult, among whom are albinos, hunchbacks, and cripples. *Bata* and *dundun* drums are played by professional drummers. *Dundun* are used for signaling—they are the "talking drums"—but they are also used by the cult of *Egungun*, younger brother of the powerful *Shango*. *Bata* are sacred to the god *Shango* (the thunder god) and his wife *Ova*, but may be played for other deities as well, and each deity has its characteristic rhythms.

Several types of aerophones (wind instruments) are of great interest. Horns are common in various parts of Negro Africa. They are made of natural horn, wood, or ivory, and are used for music as well as signaling. They usually have no finger hole or valve mechanism and only the open or natural tones can be played. In recent times, however, finger holes seem to have been introduced. One characteristic of African horns is the position of the mouthpiece or hole used for blowing, which is frequently on the side of the instrument rather than at the small end, as is common in European horns. One use of horns that produce only one pitch is in the *hocket* technique, in which each horn plays only when its note is supposed to appear in the melody.

Flutes are also frequently without finger holes, and they are sometimes used for performance in the *hocket* technique in a fashion similar to horns. This is done particularly by Negro tribes of South Africa. Ensembles of flutes with finger holes are also found, as among the Mambuti pygmies of the Congo, who use as many as six flutes, each of which varies its own short ostinato figure. The flutes are most commonly true flutes rather than the plugged flutes like the recorder. Both end-blown and transverse flutes are found, the former being held vertically. Panpipes are also present in most of Negro Africa, but little is known of the music that they produce.

Many instruments have very specific and restricted uses. Thus

[7] William Bascom, notes accompanying the record, *Drums of the Yoruba of Nigeria*, Folkways P441.

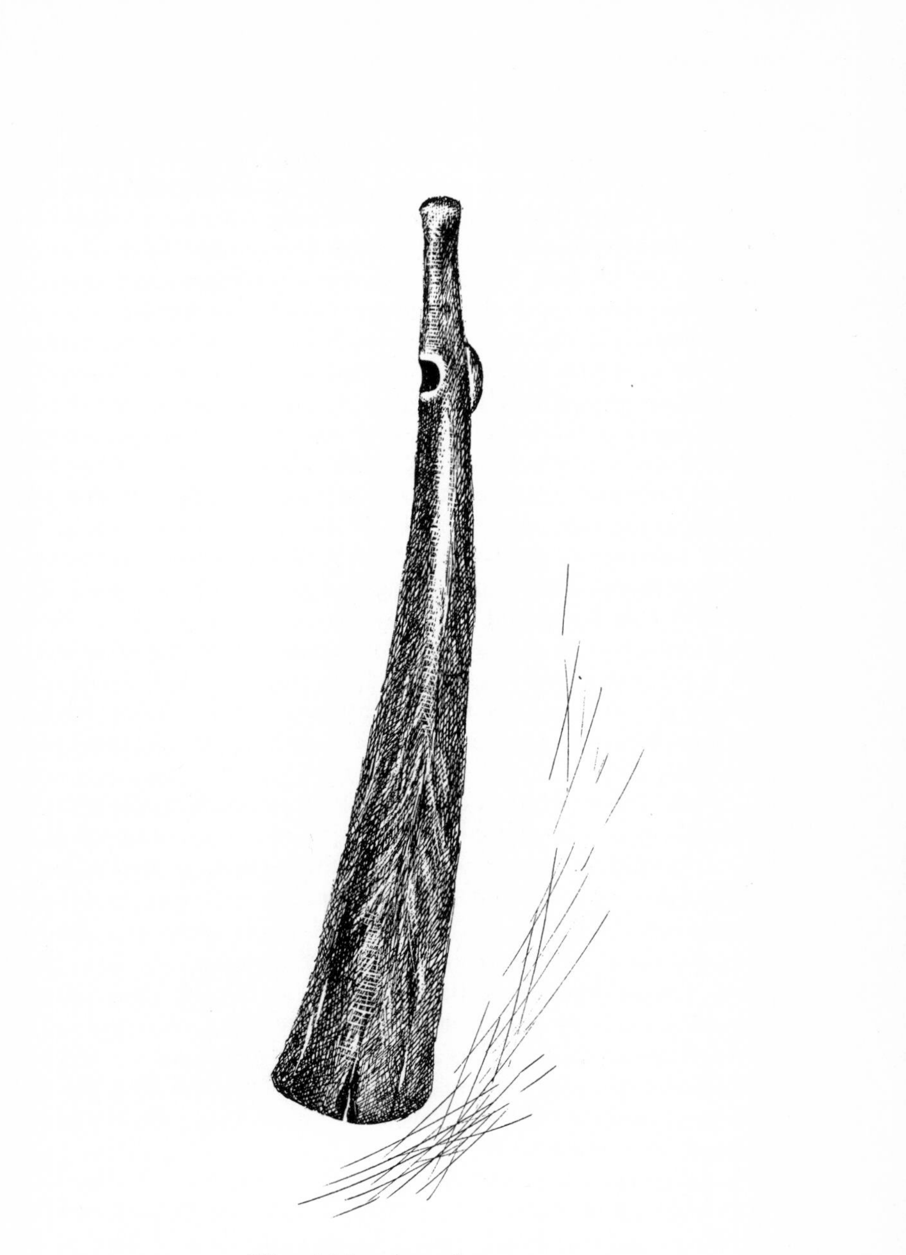

West African ivory horn.

the *epudi,* a kind of ocarina used by the Basongye of Kasai, is associated with hunting. It accompanies hunters' songs before and after the hunt, and it is used as a signaling device during the hunt. It has one finger hole and produces two tones, about a major second apart. Its major use in signaling is for reproduction of the tones of the language in ways similar to drum and horn signaling techniques.[8]

Africa has developed a large number of chordophones, or string instruments. The simplest is the musical bow, which normally has only one string but sometimes produces fairly complex music. It is found through Negro Africa, but evidently has more forms in Southeast Africa than elsewhere. It is shaped essentially like a hunting bow whose string is plucked or struck with a stick, and its sound is soft. Thus a resonator is almost always required. It may be attached to the end of the bow, or to its middle. In the latter case, the string is usually stopped at the point at which the resonator is attached, so that two strings, with contrasting pitch, are in effect used. If the resonator is not attached, the bow may be held against an inverted pot. A third way of producing resonance is for the player to hold the end of the bow in his mouth, which then acts as the resonator. If he changes the shape of his mouth, different overtones can be heard. The bow is used as a solo instrument as well as an accompaniment to song.

There has evidently been a development from the musical bow, through single-string fiddles and lutes, to more complex stringed instruments such as zithers and harps. The shapes, arrangements, and tunings of these are almost innumerable. For example, the Ganda of Uganda tune their harps into five roughly equal intervals, each about 240 cents (100 cents equal a tempered semitone) or five quarter tones. The *lulanga* of the Bashi (Congo), a trough zither in which eight strings are stretched along a concave block of wood between two and three feet long, has a tuning using mainly major and minor seconds. Frequently the tuning of instruments and thus the music produced on them seem to have little relationship to the intervals and scales of vocal music.

Aside from the musical bow, the most important African Negro stringed instruments are zithers (with several strings stretched across a board or hollowed-out block), harps (usually with four to eight strings), and fiddles (with one to five strings).

[8] Alan P. Merriam, "The Epudi, a Basongye Ocarina," *Ethnomusicology* VI (1962), 175-77.

Central African musical bow, played with mouth as resonator.

Regional variation in African Negro music

We have noted the fact that each African tribe has its own songs and music, and that each tribe may differ in its musical style from its neighbors. On the other hand, we have also given a number of characteristics present in African Negro music as a whole. The point is, of course, that these characteristics are not equally pronounced in each tribe or each area. Just as there are culture areas in Africa there are also music areas, regions in which the musical style is more or less homogeneous, and which contrast with their neighboring areas in some specific way. The music areas coincide, on the whole, with the culture areas, and this is not surprising when we consider the essential roles of music in the culture as a whole. Thus, Merriam[9] recognizes the following music areas: the Khoi-San area (Bushmen and Hottentots), East Africa, Central Africa (mainly the Congo region), the West Coast, plus several areas in the northern part of the continent that are largely under the influence of Islamic musical culture. The four areas we have mentioned comprise the main body of African Negro music. To them should be added the style of the Pygmies, who live in various isolated parts of central Africa surrounded by Negro groups, but whose music is a distinctive unit. The differences among these groups are expressed not in clear-cut dichotomies but rather in statistical terms. What may be found in one area is also present in another, but perhaps with a markedly different degree of frequency, or complexity.

The main characteristics of the West Coast are the metronome sense and the accompanying concept of "hot rhythm," the simultaneous use of several meters, and the responsorial form of singing with overlap between leader and chorus. The Central African area is distinguished by its great variety of instruments and musical styles and by the emphasis, in polyphony, on the interval of the third. East Africa has, for centuries, been somewhat under Islamic influence, though by no means to as great an extent as the northern half of Africa. Vertical fifths are more prominent here, and rhythmic structure is not so complex, nor are percussion instruments so prominent. The Khoi-San music area is evidently similar in style to East

[9] Merriam, "African Music," p. 77.

Africa, but has simpler forms and instruments. It contains a good deal of music performed with the *hocket* technique, as does the Pygmy sub-area of Central Africa, which is also characterized by the presence of a vocal technique similar to yodeling.

We have been describing those aspects of African Negro music which seem to have developed without influence from other cultures, or of which Africans have made a specialty. But outside influence is not just a recent phenomenon in African music. Thus, it shares some traits with European folk music, indicating perhaps a period of contact many centuries ago. The contact with Indonesian music seems likely, and the influence of the Near East and possibly of India is ancient and has increased greatly in the last few centuries. Western culture has also played a part for centuries and has grown especially in the last hundred years. Thus we find African music now —and it has probably always been this way to a degree—in a state of change, and it is both difficult and perhaps useless to try to single out unchanged elements. On the contrary, it behooves us to observe the changes as they take place, for this is the way to study music as a living phenomenon. We find that some tribes have almost completely changed to music in a Near Eastern style. We find that others have retained, in part, a repertory of uninfluenced African music but have added to it songs in an Arabic style; this is true of the Watusi, who have solo drumming of a kind unknown in the Near East, but who also have songs strongly reminiscent of Arabic music. We find North and Latin American popular songs known in tribes that otherwise perform aboriginal songs. And we find that because of the improvement of communication and transportation as well as through the growth of unified African nations on a supratribal level, African tribal groups are learning more from each other, musically and otherwise, than they did before. Finally, we find African composers of popular song fashioning music in the Western styles, but subtly retaining certain African elements. Surely Negro Africa will remain, as it has been in the past, musically one of the most fascinating regions of the world.

Bibliography and discography

Several publications by Alan P. Merriam discuss sub-Saharan African music as a unit: "African Music" in *Continuity and Change in African Cultures* edited by William J. Bascom and Melville J. Herskovits

(Chicago: University of Chicago Press, 1958); "Characteristics of African Music," *J-IFMC*, XI (1959), 13-19; and "The African Idiom in Music," *Journal of American Folklore*, LXXV (1962), 120-30. George Herzog, "Speech-Melody and Primitive Music," *Musical Quarterly*, XX (1934), 452-66 is an excellent discussion of tone languages and their relationship to music. Regional studies of African music are not numerous. As samples we mention J. H. Kwabena Nketia, *African Music in Ghana* (Evanston, Ill.: Northwestern University Press, 1963), for West Africa; and Rose Brandel, *The Music of Central Africa* (The Hague: M. Nijhoff, 1962), for Central Africa. Sir Percival Kirby, *The Musical Instruments of the Native Races of South Africa* (London: Oxford University Press, 1934) is a classic on the instruments and their musical styles in one area. A book profusely illustrated, dealing with instruments, is Bertil Söderberg, *Les Instruments de Musique au Bas-Congo et dans les Régions Avoisinantes* (Stockholm: Ethnographic Museum of Sweden, 1956).

Many excellent records of African music are available. A survey is presented on *Africa South of the Sahara*, edited by Harold Courlander, Folkways FE 4503 (2 disks). South and East Africa are represented on a constantly growing set of records, now already over 200 disks in number, published by the International Library of African Music, Johannesburg: *The Sound of Africa*. It is accompanied by detailed notes on a large set of catalog cards.

The Central African area is well presented on *Voice of the Congo*, edited by Alan P. Merriam, Riverside RLP 4002; *Music of Equatorial Africa*, Folkways P 402; *Folk Music of the Western Congo*, Folkways P 427; and *Songs of the Watutsi*, Folkways P 428. A record showing the elaborate drum techniques of West Africa is *Drums of the Yoruba of Nigeria*, Folkways P 441.

8

The American Indians

The American continents possess a great wealth of traditional music. Some of it, that of the Indians, has been in existence here for a long time. Another part of it, on the other hand, has been brought from other continents—mainly Europe—and preserved intact. Some, again, has developed as an offshoot of these imported foreign traditions; and some has resulted from the combination of separate traditions on American soil. Finally, some has come about independently, through the particular character and values of the American cultures, with relatively little stimulation from older traditions. It seems most sensible to discuss the folk and ethnic music of the Americas from three views: 1) the Indian, which is a tradition relatively little disturbed by the influx of other musics; 2) the Negro, which is a result of the combinations, in varying degrees, of African with European styles; and 3) the folk music of the European immigrant groups—English, Spanish, Portuguese, German, French, etc.—which have both retained archaic materials and developed new forms.

There is little doubt any more that the American Indians came from Asia, across the Bering Straits, in several or many separate waves, beginning some 50,000 years ago; that they are Mongoloid in race; and that the simplest tribes were pushed to the edges of the area (Tierra del Fuego, for example) and into relatively undesirable spots such as the jungles of Brazil and Bolivia, the Great Basin area of Nevada and Utah, and the tundra of Northern Canada and the icy wastes of the Polar area. While we realize that in 50,000 years there must have occurred a great deal of change in the styles and uses of Indian music, and while we know practically nothing about the music of East Asia of thousands of years ago, it is still possible to discover certain similarities between Indian and Oriental music, and especially between the musics of the Eskimos and of the Paleo-Siberian tribes living in easternmost Siberia. These similarities involve emphasis on melody rather than on polyphony, some use of relatively large intervals (thirds and fourths) in the melodies, and—possibly—a rather strained, tense-sounding vocal production. On the other hand, there are many different styles and style areas in North and South America, and music of the simplest sort as well as musical cultures of great complexity are found. The latter had largely disappeared by the time ethnomusicologists became competent to deal with them and they can be studied only by archeological techniques; but some of the simplest styles are still with us. The size of the Indian population seems always to have been small; north of Mexico there were probably never more than one or two million, while South and Middle American Indians evidently never exceeded about five million. That such a small number of people developed so varied and intensive a musical culture is a fact that should inspire in the modern reader a good deal of respect. Except for the similarity among the simplest tribes in both continents, there is today a great difference between South and North American Indians as a whole: The South American tribes, for the most part, have been absorbed into the Hispanic-American cultures, to which they have contributed greatly, and whose music they have to a large degree adopted; thus, for a knowledge of their aboriginal music we must depend on a few isolated tribes. The North American tribes have generally remained more separate from their white and Negro compatriots and seem to have preserved earlier musical styles to a much greater degree. For this reason, and because South American Indian music is not yet well known, our emphasis in this chapter must be on the North American Indians.

The simplest styles—an example from Bolivia

Among some Indian tribes we find music as simple as any in the world. Melodies with only two or three tones, and with a single phrase which is repeated imprecisely many times, can be found in several areas. The Sirionó of Bolivia are an interesting example,[1] for they contradict one of the truisms often repeated about the "earliest" music: rather than fulfilling ritual functions, it seems to be used mainly for entertainment. The Sirionó have no instruments and only a few simple tunes. They sing in the evening after dark, and in the morning, in their hammocks, before beginning the day's activities. The words of the songs are evidently improvised and deal with all kinds of events, past and present, assuming in a way the role of conversation. The songs usually have descending melodic contour and are sung with a "decrescendo" as the singer's breath runs out. Curiously, it seems that each member of the tribe has one tune that is the basis of all the songs he sings. He makes up different words but uses one and the same tune—possibly throughout his life. Even in such a simple musical culture there are some individuals who are said to be superior singers and who teach the young people to sing. Example 8-1 illustrates a Sirionó song.

EXAMPLE 8-1. Sirionó Indian song, from Mary Key, "Music of the Sirionó (Guaranian)," *Ethnomusicology* VII (1963), 20.

[1] Mary Key, "Music of the Sirionó (Guaranian)," *Ethnomusicology* VII (1963), 17-21.

Uses of Indian music—an example from the Plains

Indian tribes with more complex kinds of musical culture usually have several types of songs, each of which is associated with different activities. For example, the Arapaho Indians of the North American Plains have ceremonial and secular songs. Among the former, the most elaborate are the songs of the Sun Dance, a ceremony performed in the summer, when the various bands of the tribe came together after being separated all winter. The Sun Dance involves the search for a vision in which the individual warrior receives a guardian spirit. The vision is brought on by self-torture and by dancing around a pole while looking at the bright sun for hours. With the exception of the Ghost Dance and Peyote songs (which are discussed below), all of the Arapaho songs are very much alike; they consist of two sections, each descending in a terrace-like contour; they have a range of over an octave and scales of four, five, or six tones; and they are sung with great tension on the vocal chords and with rhythmic pulsations on the long notes. Even though they sound much alike, the various types of songs have certain individual characteristics. Thus the Sun Dance songs are a bit longer than the rest, have a slightly larger average range (about a twelfth), and their final phrase, in the last repetition at a performance of a song, is sung by the women alone. Songs learned in visions are another type, and songs belonging to the various age-grade societies, a third. (Each man was a member of one of seven age-grade societies, with elaborate initiations and with particular duties in war, and as he aged he was promoted from one society to the next.) Among the secular songs, we may mention various types of social dance songs—the snake dance, turtle dance, round dance, and rabbit dance. Each has minor characteristics distinguishing it: The round dance songs are usually in rollicking triple meter; the rabbit dance—danced by couples and evidently introduced after contact with the whites—has songs that ordinarily begin with descending fourths. And there are war songs intended to inspire warriors, and others used to recount events in recent battles. There are also songs said to be taught by the guardian spirit, and which the recipient is to sing only when he is near death. Also, there are children's songs, lullabies, and love songs.

Finally we must mention two types of songs recognized as separate types by the Arapaho and by other Plains tribes, the Peyote and Ghost Dance songs. The Ghost Dance is a religion that was introduced in the 1880's by tribes further west, in the Great Basin of Nevada; it was a cult, outlawed by the U.S.A. in 1891, which preached war and annihilation to the encroaching whites, a last-ditch stand against the inevitable. The Ghost Dance movement brought with it, from the Great Basin, a musical style different from that of the older Plains songs. Typically its songs had a smaller range and a form in which each phrase is repeated once, for instance, AABB or AABBCC. Among the Plains Indians, such as the Arapaho, these songs came to be associated with the Ghost Dance religion, and when the dance was outlawed, the songs continued to be sung. Their style was also associated with hand games and gambling games. Another musical style was brought to the Arapaho and other Plains Indians by the Peyote religion. Peyote, a cactus indigenous in Mexico, has buttons which when chewed have a mild narcotic effect, producing euphoria and eventually pleasant hallucinations. The Aztecs already had a cult built around Peyote, but a religion of a different sort, preaching conciliation with the whites and including some superficial elements of Christianity, was based on this drug in North America. Peyote reached some of the Apache tribes after 1700 and spread from them to the majority of tribes in the United States during the nineteenth and early twentieth centuries. The style of Peyote music is essentially the same among all of the North American tribes that use the Peyote ceremonies; and uniformly it differs from the older musical styles of those tribes. Its form is similar to that of the older Plains songs, but its rhythm is characterized by the fact that it is rapid and composed mainly of only two note values—which can be notated by quarter and eighth notes; also it is accompanied by rapid playing of the drum and rattle. Special kinds of meaningless syllables and a particular closing or cadential formula are used. Peyote songs are definitely considered as a special type by the Arapaho.

The Arapaho culture does not have as many uses of music as do some other Indian tribes. For example, the Pueblo Indians have much more complex and numerous ceremonial songs. They also use music to accompany work, something unusual among Indians. The Navaho have elaborate curing rituals accompanied by several series of songs, and a large body of corn grinding songs. The Indians of the Southeastern United States have many kinds of social dances. Throughout, music is associated with religion, and no description of a ceremony would be complete without a discussion of the songs. In most tribes, the most significant musical creations are those in the ceremonies. Among the Eskimos, some songs are used to settle disputes and to relieve tension among quarreling tribesmen.

Music in Indian thought

We have only little knowledge regarding the musical aesthetics of Indian tribes. Ability to sing many songs, and to sing high, is the mark of a good singer on the Plains; the Pueblo Indians, on the other hand, prefer singers with low, growling voices. Songs are judged according to their "power" rather than their beauty. Various ideas regarding the origin of songs are found among the North American tribes. According to some, all songs were given to the tribe in "the beginning," and the idea that new songs can be made up is not accepted. Among the Yuman tribes of the extreme Southwest, songs are thought to be "dreamed," that is, made up or given to a person while he is asleep.[2] Curiously, Yuman persons who are disturbed or emotionally maladjusted retire for a few weeks to a secluded hut, there to meditate and to "dream" songs, and they eventually emerge much improved. Among the Pima of the Southwest, we find the idea that songs already exist, and that it is the job of the composer simply to "untangle" them. Among the Plains tribes, the idea that songs come in visions is prevalent; of course all songs do not come in this way, but those which are ceremonially most significant do. The possibility of learning songs from other tribes is accepted variously; Herzog found that the Pima, who sang songs with Yuma words, would not admit that these songs could have been imported. On the other hand, Plains tribes regularly label the songs borrowed from other tribes; thus the Cheyenne Indians have "Kiowa songs" and "Comanche songs."

The degree to which songs retain their form from year to year

[2] George Herzog, "Music in the Thinking of the American Indian," *Peabody Bulletin*, May, 1933, pp. 1-6.

and from generation to generation also varies. Some tribes, such as those of the Northwest Coast, consider it important to keep a song intact. Change or error might invalidate its purpose in ritual or rob it of its power. Thus organized rehearsing was instituted and errors were punished. The attempt to retain the cultural heritage intact and the resistance to change in general is also felt, of course, in the musical culture. The Pueblo Indians, who have tended to resist change in all areas, have also kept their musical culture away from Western influence more than have some other tribes. The Plains Indians, who had a rather loose and informal political and ceremonial structure, evidently did not adhere to such standardized forms; one Arapaho informant, upon hearing a recording of one of his tribal songs, performed what he considered "the same song" by singing what seemed to the investigator a totally different melody.

Musical instruments

The instruments of the North American Indians are relatively few in number, but the Middle and South American tribes had a considerable wealth of them. In North America, flutes and various sorts of percussion instruments constitute an overwhelming majority. Flutes are usually of the recorder type, with varying numbers of finger holes; the tunes they are used to perform are frequently those of songs that are also sung. True flutes, without the plug of the recorder, also appear. In some cases, the ornamentation of the vocal line is faithfully reproduced on the flute; in others, the flute embellishes the tune. Flutes are most frequently used to play love songs, and they are played almost exclusively by men. Whistles of various sorts, made of bone, pottery, or wood, are used in conjunction with songs and ceremonies. Drums and rattles are the main percussion instruments of North America. Drums are usually beaten with sticks rather than the hand, and they (as well as the rattles) are used only to accompany song. Most Indian drums have a single drumhead; some are so large that they can be played by several players simultaneously. Some are held in on hand, the player grasping the leather thongs that hold the skin against the rim. Kettledrums, sometimes filled with water, are used. The Peyote ceremony requires such a drum, whose drumhead is moistened so that it has what the player

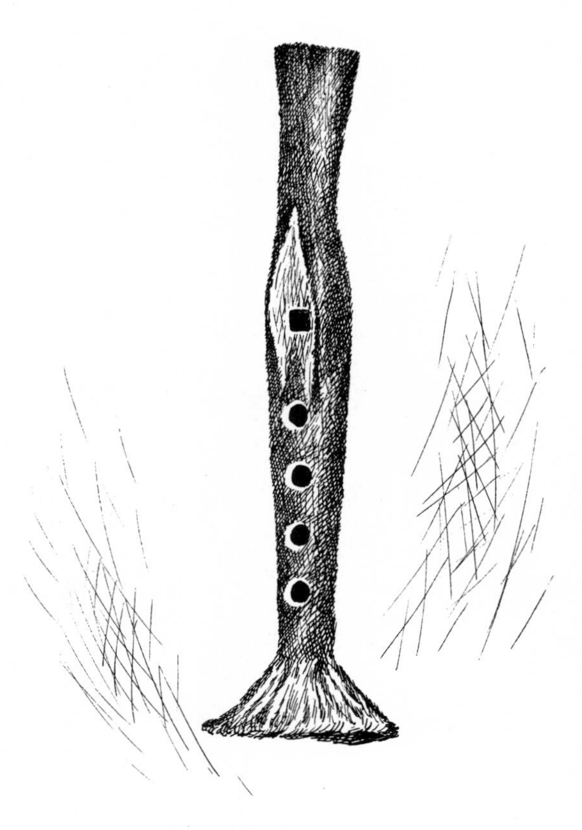

Ancient Mexican clay flute.

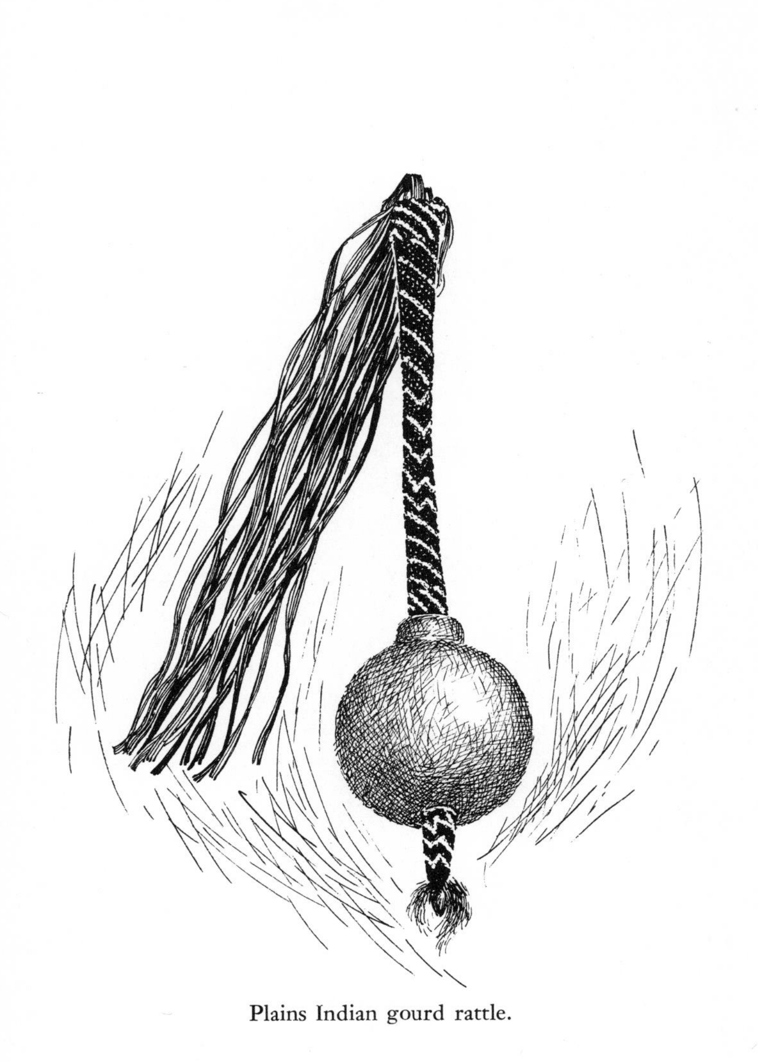

Plains Indian gourd rattle.

considers the appropriate pitch. Typically, each drum is associated with one or several specific ceremonies and is an object of importance beyond its musical service.

Rattles are also of various types and associated with specific ceremonies. Gourd rattles (with pebbles inside the gourd) are used for Peyote ceremonies. Also used in North America are rattles made of deer hooves strung together; rattles made on a base consisting of a turtle shell; notched sticks held against a basket resonator and rubbed with another stick; and wooden bells. The South American Indians have a larger variety of rattles, but they are particularly distinguished from the North American tribes in the development of panpipes and of chordophones (string instruments). Panpipes made of fired clay and of wood have evidently been used in the highlands of Peru and Bolivia for centuries. Some are made of pipes up to five feet tall. The number and arrangement of pipes varies, but, interestingly enough, this type of instrument has been altered and its scale made to fit Western popular music, so that some of the present-day Indians of Peru, for example, use them to play tunes in the prevalent Hispanic style. While there is inconclusive evidence that some North American tribes used hunting bows to play simple tunes, the musical bow, played in much the same ways as in Africa, appears among several South American tribes, including the simple Araucanians of Patagonia. The high cultures of Peru, Colombia, and Mexico had rather elaborate instruments of various sorts, but we know little about the music produced on them.

Styles by area in North America

The distribution of musical styles among the North American Indians coincides more or less with that of the culture areas. There appears to be, however, a somewhat smaller degree of correspondence here than there is in Africa. South American Indian music is not yet sufficiently well known for us to construct musical areas. In North America (north of Mexico) there are six main areas; in some cases these cannot be distinguished on the basis of single pieces of music, and the distinctions among them are statistical, that is, they depend on the frequency of a given trait rather than its simple presence or absence.

1) The Northwest Coast-Eskimo area contains, besides the areas mentioned, the Salish Indians in the interior of British Columbia and in the state of Washington. While these groups have little in common culturally, they seem to be among the most recent immigrants from Asia. Their music is characterized by nonstrophic forms, by complex and sometimes nonmetrical rhythmic organization, by the prominence of small intervals such as minor seconds, and by a relatively small range in the melodies. The melodic contours in Eskimo music tend to be undulating, while they are more frequently of a pendulum type in Northwest Coast and Salish music. One important characteristic is the use of rhythmic motifs in the percussive accompaniment. Generally, in Indian music, drums and rattles follow a simple pulse. But in the Northwest Coast-Eskimo area, simple designs such as ♪ ♪> ♪ 𝄽 or ♪ ♩> ♪ are found. In spite of the unity, however, the Eskimo music is generally simple while that of the Northwest is complex and, in its relative wealth of instruments, indicates some relationship to the culture of the Mexican civilizations.

2) The California-Yuman area, consisting of tribes in Central California and of the Yuman-speaking tribes of the extreme Southwestern United States, is characterized by singing in a relatively relaxed manner. Most Indian tribes use a tense, harsh vocal technique, but here the singing is more in the style of Western or Central European folk singing. The songs are not in strophic form, that is, they consist not simply of a repetition of the basic form, but rather of two or more separate sections or phrases which are repeated, alternated, and interwoven without a predetermined pattern. The most characteristic feature of this area is the so-called rise, a form discovered and labeled by George Herzog.[3] The rise itself is a section of a song that is slightly higher in pitch than the rest of the song. Its average pitch or tessitura is higher, but sometimes not very obviously so. Yet the Yuman Indians recognize this feature and use a word roughly translated as "rise" to indicate it. The rise is found in most songs of the Yuman-California area, but it is also found elsewhere, mainly along the coasts of North America. Thus, it is found in some 20 or 30 per cent of the songs of some Northwest Coast tribes, and in those of the Southeastern Choctaw; in 10 to 20 per cent of the songs of the

[3] George Herzog, "The Yuman Musical Style," *Journal of American Folklore* LXI (1928), 183-231.

Northwestern Penobscot and the Northwestern Nootka, and in less than 10 per cent of the repertory of the Southeastern Creek, Yuchi, and Tutelo.

3) A third area is centered in the Great Basin of Nevada, Utah, and northern interior California, basically a desert area with simple hunting and gathering cultures. The style of the music here became the style of the Ghost Dance songs further to the East. Singing is in a relatively relaxed manner, melodic range is small, and the typical form is that of paired phrases, with each phrase repeated once. In the northwestern part of the area, some tribes with even a simpler style—the Modoc and Klamath, for example—have many songs consisting of a single repeated phrase. This kind of form is found, of course, in traditional musics throughout the world, and there are a few Indian tribes such as the previously mentioned Sirionó of Bolivia whose entire repertories don't go beyond this level of simplicity. But it seems possible that the simple repetitive forms of the Modoc and Klamath are historically related to the somewhat more complex but still essentially repetitive forms of the Great Basin proper. Because of long-standing contacts with the Plains Indians, the Great Basin tribes also have songs in the Plains style. And an interesting exception to the tendency of Indian songs to be short and to eschew narration is the existence, among the Ute, of some songs that serve as the vehicle for reciting tales. These narrative songs do not have strophic forms (as do European ballads), but continue in unstructured fashion, liberally repeating and varying a few basic musical motifs. Example 8-2 illustrates the Great Basin style.

4) A fourth area, the Athabascan, seems to coincide with a language family by the same name. It consists of the Navaho and Apache tribes and—possibly—of another group of tribes, the Northern Athabascans, in Western Canada. Though these northern tribes have for centuries been separated from the Navaho and Apache by a thousand miles, there is evidence that the musical styles of the two areas are related. The music of the Navaho is the most complex of this area, perhaps because it has been greatly influenced by the neighboring Pueblo tribes. Its melodies have a large range, a pendulum-like melodic movement, large intervals, and liberal use of falsetto. The Apache songs tend to have smaller range and tenser singing. What ties them together is the form—it is usually nonstrophic and resembles that of the California-Yuman tribes—and the rhythmic struc-

EXAMPLE 8-2. Paiute Indian song, from George Herzog, "Plains Ghost Dance and Great Basin Music," *American Anthropologist* XXXVII (1935), 419.

ture, in which meter is rather well established but change of meter is frequent and sudden. The note values in each song are few, usually just two—quarters and eighths—and it seems likely that the style of Peyote music, as described for the Arapaho above, is in this respect based on the music of the Apache, from whom the use of Peyote for ceremonies had spread to the other tribes. Example 8-3 is a Navaho song.

5) The Plains-Pueblo area takes in two of the most important cultural groups, the Plains Indians (Blackfoot, Crow, Dakota, Comanche, Kiowa, etc.) and the Pueblo Indians. The most recent aboriginal form of living of the Plains Indians was nomadic; their economy was based on the buffalo. Their loose political and ceremonial structure contrasts with the elaborate organization of life and religion among the Pueblo Indians (Hopi, Zuni, Taos, etc.), and there has in recent centuries been only slight contact among these two groups. Yet their music shares some important characteristics, particularly the great amount of tension in the singing and the two-part song form, which was described above for the Arapaho. The use of terrace-like melodic contour, gradually descending and leveling off on a long, low tone, is also typical (although the Pueblo songs often precede this form with a low-pitched introduction). The area directly east of the Plains, including such tribes as the Pawnee

EXAMPLE 8-3. Navaho Indian Enemy Way ceremony song, from David P. McAllester, *Enemy Way Music* (Cambridge, Mass.: Peabody Museum Papers 49, no. 3, 1954), song no. 35.

and the Eastern Woodland tribes such as the Menomini, Chippewa, and Winnebago, shares the main traits of the Plains, but adds some characteristic ones of its own. Typically the Plains songs do not have strongly pronounced metric units, nor are repeated rhythmic patterns or motifs usually evident. Among the tribes to the east, however, repeated rhythmic motifs can be identified, and a good many songs have elements of isorhythmic form—a rhythmic pattern is repeated several times, with different melodic content each time. Of course, this practice is also found here and there among the typical Plains tribes. Example 8-4 presents an Arapaho song.

6) The eastern portion of the United States and Southern Canada may be considered as one musical area, although it is only sporadically known. Perhaps the most distinctive feature is the de-

Song is repeated four times. Drum begins before the singers.
* Women enter here in repeat.
⊕ During last rendition, women finish alone, without drum.

EXAMPLE 8-4. Arapaho Sun Dance song, from Bruno Nettl, *Musical Culture of the Arapaho* (M. A. thesis, Indiana University, 1951), p. 100.

velopment of responsorial singing—shouts thrown back and forth between leader and chorus, probably as a result of rudimentary rounds. Forms are frequently elaborate and composed of several phrases, some of which recur. Thus, the Eagle Dance ceremony of the Iroquois has many songs with the form AABAB, in which section A is always accompanied by quick shaking of the rattle, while B has slower percussive accompaniment. Similarly, some of the southeastern tribes have social dances accompanied by groups of songs strung together in series that are repeated and interwoven in intricate sequences. Vocal technique is tense, and melodic contour usually descending, though not in the predictable terrace patterns of the Plains. The tribes living in the Gulf of Mexico area seem to have had, before the advent of the whites, a very complex culture related to that of the Aztecs, and it is possible that their music was similarly more complex. But little of this remains. Example 8-5 is an Iroquois song, an example of music from the eastern area.

The level of musical complexity among these areas varies. Pueblo, eastern, and Northwest Coast are the most complex and developed, while the Great Basin is, on the whole, the simplest. Although the musical areas do not correspond precisely to the culture areas, they do coincide at various major points. Such easily defined culture areas as the Plains and the Northwest Coast have a unified musical style. The greatest cultural diversity as well as the greatest

EXAMPLE 8-5. Iroquois thanksgiving ritual song, from Wallace Chafe, *Seneca Thanksgiving Rituals* (Washington, D.C.: Bureau of American Ethnology, Bulletin 183, 1961), p. 66.

musical variety is found in the western part of the continent. On the other hand, the large number of language families found in North America do not coincide in their geographic distribution with either the musical or the culture areas.

Indian music of Latin America

It is interesting to find some of the North American stylistic traits paralleled in South America. This is true of the terrace-shaped melodic contours of the Plains tribes, which are found also among tribes in Northern Argentina. But in contrast to North America, the South American Indians seem to have developed some polyphony to the level of definite intention; thus, the tribes of Tierra del Fuego occasionally sing in parallel fifths.

The Latin American area produced several Indian cultures

whose technology and whose social and political organization were considerably higher than those of most nonliterate tribes, and which were comparable perhaps to some of the ancient civilizations of Europe and Asia. We are speaking, of course, of the Mayas of the Yucatan peninsula (who developed a kind of written communication), the Aztecs, and some of their predecessors, the Inca of Peru, and the Chibcha of Colombia. Little of their musical culture has remained, but there is archeological evidence to support the belief that they had rather elaborate musical practices and styles. Their instruments were larger in number—though not much more complex—than those of other tribes. Pictorial representations of groups of instrumentalists indicate that playing in ensembles was a common practice. The Mexican cultures, though together they span hundreds of years, seem to have used essentially the same instruments: Prominent were the *teponatzli*, a log drum with a slit similar to some of the West African signal drums; the *tlapitzalli* (our names here are the Nahuatl forms—this is the language of the Aztecs), a true flute with four finger holes, made of clay, reed, or bone, with major seconds and minor thirds as the main intervals; the *huehuetl*, a kettle drum which was produced in several distinct sizes and pitches; a conch-shell trumpet; rattles; and rasps. The Incas added to these types a large number of ocarinas, flutes with varying numbers of finger holes (three to eight), and panpipes. The identity of tuning of some Peruvian panpipes with some of Oceania has been a factor in the debate about the possibility and nature of contact between native South America and Oceania.

According to early Spanish accounts[4] of the remnants of Aztec culture, the Aztecs recognized only religious music, and musical life was largely in the hands of a professional religious caste. Some instruments themselves had divine power. Music was normally performed by groups in concert, and responsorial singing was heard. Musicians were trained rigidly, and performances had to be completely accurate in order to please the deities; errors such as missed drumbeats were punished.

Before their discovery by the Spaniards, the Inca evidently had an even more elaborate musical culture than the Aztecs. The ruler

[4] Robert Stevenson, *Music in Mexico* (New York: Thomas Y. Crowell Company, 1952), pp. 14-19.

had specially trained musicians for entertainment at his court. A school of music was instituted at Cuzco by the Inca Roca about 1350,[5] and in the fifteenth century the Inca Pachacuti ordered the collection of narrative songs about the deeds of the earlier Inca rulers; these were organized in song cycles.

The words of Indian songs

The words of Indian songs are of considerable interest, for they frequently fit into the musical structure in unexpected and interesting ways. For example, the Plains Indians, with their two-part song structure, have developed a rather dramatic but simultaneously utilitarian way of setting words to music. Most of the song is taken up with meaningless syllables, such as "he-he" or "ho-ho," but the meaningful text appears at the beginning of the second section, which starts again (as does the first) on a high note and works its way downward. Its structure does not have the characteristics–such as rime or meter–of European poetry; it is rather like prose, although meaningless syllables sometimes appear between words and even between the syllables of one word, presumably in order to keep the stressed syllables on stressed musical beats. The text does not cover the whole second part of the song, and when it is finished, the meaningless syllables are again used to fill in the rest of the melody. This kind of structure gives considerable flexibility to the composer or poet, for it enables him to substitute new words for old in the same tune, or to make slight changes in the words in order to keep up with the times. Thus, warriors of the Plains would report on their exploits in such songs, and the same tune could be used for various exploits. After World War I, in which many Indians served as soldiers, old tunes with new words recounting stories of the war began to appear. Such words as "Germany" and an Arapaho word for submarine began to appear in the songs. Frequently these songs used texts from the tribal wars, but simply substituted German soldiers for Indian tribes; for example, "The German officer ran and dragged his blanket along." The following are song texts of the Arapaho:[6]

[5] Robert Stevenson, *The Music of Peru: Aboriginal and Viceroyal Epochs* (Washington: Pan American Union, 1959), p. 39.

[6] Collected by Bruno Nettl.

Woman, don't worry about me; I'm coming back home to eat berries.
I am the crow; watch me.
The bird has come; it makes yellow the sky.
Young man, be brave; you're going to a dangerous place; your chieftainship will become famous.
Really it is good to be young, for old age is not far off.
The Ute Indian, while he was still looking around for me, I scalped him alive.
Young man, it is good that you are going to war.

Elsewhere among the North American Indians, however, meaningless syllables are not so prevalent, and entire tunes are accompanied by words; the subjects range from serious thoughts about the gods to lyrical complaints about the weather, to frivolous love songs. But the meaningless syllable songs occupy an important role, analogous perhaps to instrumental music. Thus there are entire bodies of song that use meaningless syllables. The famous night chant of the Navaho, the "yeibetchai," includes a group of songs sung by masked dancers in falsetto with only syllables. Many of the Peyote songs use only meaningless words, but, interestingly enough, they use special patterns such as "yowitsini," "heyowitsi," and "heyowitsinayo," which can easily be identified as Peyote songs. Some of the Indian texts are long and elaborate; the Navaho songs may enumerate holy people, places, or things in great numbers. More commonly, however, a short sentence or phrase is repeated several times.

Indian music in transition

Considering the small number of Indians and the tremendous impact of Western culture on their lives during the past two or three centuries, it would be surprising if their music had remained uninfluenced by that of the West. There is an interesting difference between North and Latin American cultures in this regard. The Indians of Latin America, who in several countries now make up the bulk of the Spanish-speaking population, have learned the folk music styles of Spain and have also developed styles that are to an extent mixed. Thus it is possible to hear, in the Andes of Peru, tunes in the Hispanic folk music style being played on the panpipe, an aboriginal Indian instrument. In North America—probably mainly because the Indians have been segregated—such a mixture of styles did not take place. There are occasional exceptions, of course, as in the case of Peyote songs being accompanied by piano. Some North American Indians, moreover, learned songs from the white folk and popular repertory, but unlike the American Negroes, they did not create a style consisting of elements from both sides, Indian and white. This may perhaps be attributed to the great difference between Indian and European musical styles, in contrast to the relatively greater similarity of the Western and African musics. But we should not rule out subtle influences; for example, in the Plains, the intervals of Peyote songs seem to coincide more frequently with those of European music than do those of the older song types. If this is so, the more recently introduced Peyote song style (in retrospect) would be more easily subject to foreign influence because presumably the influence occurred at the time the style was being formed.

The influence of the West can also be felt in less direct ways in American Indian music. In Mexico and Peru, the relatively high developments in musical culture were reduced to simpler levels and styles through the annihilation or reduction of the ruling classes, and through the introduction of Christianity. In Central America, the presence of simple, xylophone-like instruments facilitated the introduction of the African *marimba.* In North America, where homogeneous styles evidently had been developed and musical areas of some stability had been formed aboriginally, the encroachment of the whites and the resulting migration of tribes caused a greater degree of intertribal contact than had previously been known. Tribes with radically different musical cultures became neighbors and learned from each other. An example is the Shawnee tribe, which at the time of first white contact was located in the southeastern United States, but which within a few centuries had probably come from the Northeast. It participated in the music of the eastern musical area, but was forced to migrate westward and was located in Oklahoma, near some of the Plains tribes. Its repertory today contains songs in both the Plains and the eastern styles, as well as simple songs of an old layer which they may have brought with them from the Northeast, and the Peyote style, to which they were introduced only in the twentieth century. The spreading of the Peyote and Ghost Dance styles to tribes with other kinds of music was, of course, also the result—indirect, perhaps—of the impact of Western culture. Another way in which the whites have influenced Indian music indirectly is through the gradual impoverishment of the repertories, and a changing emphasis from ceremonial song to social, dance, and love songs. Indian songs with English words are frequently found; the forms of the songs in some areas such as the Plains have been simplified or shortened; and songs now consist of fewer sections and more limited scales.

As tribes are thrown together, and as the older tribal culture disappears, the Indians of the United States are making conscious efforts to preserve their heritage. One method is to ignore tribal distinctions and to work toward a musical tradition that is acceptable to members of many tribes and areas. This method has been used, in part unconsciously because of the obliteration of tribal identities and in part consciously by those who would preserve Indian culture, in the creation of pan-Indian ceremonies and social events. Festivals, such as that in Gallup, New Mexico (and there are dozens of similar events throughout the country each summer), allow the members of one tribe to present their songs and dances to those of other tribes. In areas in which there are few Indians, members of several tribes cooperate in presenting musical and dance events. In some American cities, scattered Indians will frequently join in a pan-Indian association one of whose functions is the sponsorship of such events. One result has been the growing tendency of all Indians to learn and sing songs in a single style; thus we have had the gradual development of a pan-Indian musical style that is largely based on the music of the Plains-Pueblo area, in somewhat simplified form. To some extent the style is determined by the preferences of the white spectators, who seem to consider the Plains style as the most typically "Indian" music. The development of pan-Indian styles of music is an interesting example of the way in which musical culture is tied to the developments of culture in general. And it is a poignant illustration of the importance of traditional music to a people whose traditional culture is nearing extinction.

Bibliography and discography

Since this chapter, besides covering American Indian music, also introduces the music of the Americas generally, some publications on the entire subject are given here. Charles Haywood, *A Bibliography of North American Folklore and Folksong*, rev. ed. (New York: Dover,

1961, 2 vols.) and Gilbert Chase, *A Guide to the Music of Latin America*, 2nd ed. (Washington: Pan American Union, 1962) are indispensable bibliographies. Bruno Nettl, *An Introduction to Folk Music in the United States* (Detroit: Wayne State University Press, 1960) is a brief survey.

Two attempts to show the various styles in North American Indian music are Helen H. Roberts, *Musical Areas in Aboriginal North America* (New Haven: Yale University Press, 1936) and Bruno Nettl, *North American Indian Musical Styles* (Philadelphia: American Folklore Society, 1954). The most prolific author on North American Indian music was Frances Densmore, and all of her publications, many of them published by the Bureau of American Ethnology, Smithsonian Institution, Washington, D.C., are worth examination. Recent developments in this field are discussed by Willard Rhodes, "Acculturation in North American Indian Music," in *Acculturation in the Americas*, ed. Sol Tax (Chicago: University of Chicago Press, 1952). Robert Stevenson, *The Music of Peru, Aboriginal and Viceroyal Epochs* (Washington: Pan American Union, 1959) devotes two chapters to what is known of ancient Inca music. Karl G. Izikowitz, *Musical and Other Sound Instruments of the South American Indians* (Göteborg: Elanders, 1935) is a comprehensive discussion of its field.

The Library of Congress has issued a number of recordings made from Frances Densmore's collections in its series, *Folk Music of the United States*. Another series covering many tribes is *Music of the American Indian*, edited by Willard Rhodes, Library of Congress AAFS L34-43.

Other recordings of North American Indian music of interest are *Indian Music of the Canadian Plains*, Folkways P 464; *American Indians of the Southwest*, Folkways FW 8850; and *Music of the Sioux and Navaho*, Folkways P 401. Indian music of Latin America is presented in *Indian Music of Mexico*, Folkways P 413; *Music from Mato Grosso*, Folkways P 446; and *Indian Music of the Upper Amazon*, Folkways P 458.

9

Negro Folk Music in the New World

One of the truly important musical developments in modern world history was caused by the largely forced migration of great numbers of African Negroes to various parts of the Americas. These slaves, most of whom came from West Africa, brought with them their music and other features of their culture, which served to provide a common context for the partial continuation, at least, of the African traditions. The Negroes came into contact with European music of varying styles; their reactions to these styles and the resulting mixture of musics called into being a whole group of musical subcultures that have had an impact on all strata of twentieth-century music.

Not only are the folk musics of the various Negro communities in the New World intrinsically interesting and alive, but they have influenced the folk music of the whites as well, to the extent of having played a major role in the development of some of the typical North and Latin American musical forms; they are responsible for the character of a good deal of Western popular music; their importance in the development of jazz is well known; and their effect on the composers of art music, beginning with Dvořák (1841-1904) and Gershwin (1898-1937) all the way to William Grant Still (1895-1964) and Ulysses S. Kay (b. 1917), is considerable.

The origins of the New World Negro styles

The origin of the New World Negro styles has been a subject of much debate over the past century. Extreme views—the music is actually African, unchanged by migration; or the music is simply a copy of Western form and style; the American Negro is a superlatively creative individual; or he is capable of creating nothing but the simplest spontaneous musical utterances—have frequently been published. A more moderate view is now generally accepted. According to the kind of thinking to which American anthropologists of the 1960's subscribe, the slaves did indeed bring their African songs and pieces. In those areas in which they outnumbered their white neighbors and masters, and where they were isolated from the whites, they retained this African music with relatively little change. Elsewhere they actually learned the songs of the whites. Everywhere, however, they were influenced by the music of the whites (and in cases by that of the Indians), and they modified their own way of singing to some extent in accordance with that of the whites. Thus their musical acculturation takes three possible forms: they may simply learn the songs of the whites with their performance practices; they may learn the performance practices of the whites and superimpose these on their own songs; or, conversely, they may learn the songs of the whites and superimpose on them the African performance practices.

All of these things happened to some degree. The Negroes of the United States learned songs from their white masters, from missionaries, and from neighbors in the cities. Some of these songs were sung in styles indistinguishable from those of the whites, but on most of them the Negroes imposed some stylistic traits from Africa. They presumably also continued to sing African songs and to compose new songs in the African styles, but this was problematic because the slaves did not have a common language and tribal groups were purposely broken up by the slave traders. The African elements that were retained were among those also found in similar form in European folk or popular music, for according to the theory of syncretism stated by Waterman,[1] cultural features that have something in common are likely to merge into a new though related form in an acculturational situation.

Just what are the African features that were carried into the New World? The emphasis on rhythm is an important one, and it is expressed in the frequent use of percussion instruments and in rhythmic accompaniment, as well as in the tendency to adhere strictly to meter and tempo (the "metronome sense" of West Africans), and, perhaps as a result, in the use of syncopation and of complicated rhythmic figures. A second one is the call-and-response pattern, antiphonally and responsorially performed. The love of instruments and instrumental music—though the instruments themselves are frequently quite different from those of Africa—among New World Negro groups may be a result of the wealth of instruments in Africa. The interest in improvisation is also perhaps one of the African features, as is the tendency to use a variety of tone colors in the vocal technique—especially harsh, throaty singing. Finally, polyphonic singing, though it is not particularly typical of either West African or New World Negro music, may, where it is found, perhaps be traced to African roots.

It is frequently difficult to decide whether a feature of New World Negro music is part of the African heritage. As we have pointed out, these features may have maintained themselves in a hostile cultural environment only because their counterparts in Western folk and popular music were somewhat similar. But it is interesting to find that, on the whole, those features of music which were most strongly developed in Africa have to some extent been retained in American Negro music; but those which were relatively unde-

[1] Richard A. Waterman, "African Influence on American Negro Music," in *Acculturation in the Americas,* ed. Sol Tax (Chicago: University of Chicago Press, 1952), p. 212.

veloped (or not developed in a specialized or striking direction), such as scale and form, seem to have given way and to have been replaced by features bearing the European trademark.

Anthropologists who have studied the relationship between African and American Negro cultures have often remarked on the great extent to which African features have remained in the American Negro's musical repertory. At times this fact has been ascribed to the supposedly special native musical talent of Negroes, and it has even been supposed that certain musical features (emphasis on rhythm, call-and-response, and so forth) are part of the Negro's biological heredity. The question of basic musical talent is unsolved (but it seems unlikely that any racial group would have precedence in the inheritance of such a complex group of aspects of behavior as musical talent), and several studies have shown that the inheritance of specific musical features has never been proved. The explanation is probably much simpler. Music plays an important role in African Negro life and ritual, and as such has occupied a position of high value. It is not surprising that the Africans cherished their musical heritage when they were brought to the Americas. Also, music was in several ways more complex and more highly developed in Africa than in the Indian and Western folk cultures with which the Negroes came into contact in the Americas. Finally, the Negroes have not been in the New World so very long, and it seems probable that the more Negroes were isolated as groups, the more African their music remained. Also, the more closely a piece of music or a body of songs was associated with religion or ritual, the more likely it was to have features of African styles. But only occasionally, at least in North America, do the songs have elements of African languages; and there seem to be few melodies of African origin in the New World repertories.

Among the New World Negro populations, those of Haiti, the Guianas, and Northern Brazil (especially Bahia) seem to have folk music most similar in style to that of Africa. Jamaica, Trinidad, and Cuba are next, and the United States Negro music exhibits the fewest Africanisms. Usually, the Negroes living in the cities have become more acculturated and thus have lost more of their African heritage than those living in the rural areas, especially in the United States. But this is not the case everywhere, for the large Negro populations in Brazilian cities seem to have been sufficiently cohesive to retain a greater degree of African style than have those of the surrounding farms and plantations.

When discussing the amount of African residue in American Negro music we must not forget, however, that this material has itself influenced the white and Indian repertories throughout the continents to a considerable degree, and that the Negro communities in some areas of the New World—particularly the Caribbean—provide the basic musical style on which the other groups base their musical traditions.

Negro music in Latin America

In Latin America, African musical elements are most strongly preserved in the music of various cults involving deities that have been transferred from the West African homeland and whose character has changed in the process. West African religions, typically, involve a pantheon of major and lesser deities, each of which had a cult developed about itself, with characteristic ceremonies, songs, and drum rhythms. These cults were developed further in the Americas, sometimes taking on a semi-Christian character through the assimilation of a Roman Catholic saint into the personality of the African god. And since members of different tribes and nations from Africa were often thrown together on plantations and in the cities in South America and the Caribbean, these cults sometimes became the bases and expressions of national and tribal groupings. In Bahia (Brazil), these cult groups are called *candomblé*. According to Merriam,[2] the following are among the important Bahian cult groups: *Ketu* and *Jesha* (derived from the Yoruba of Nigeria); *Congo Angola* (from the Congo area); *Gêgê* (from Dahomey); and *Caboclo, Guarani,* and *Caboclo Guarani* (derived from indigenous Indian religious beliefs and practices combined with some of those from West Africa).

In Haiti, similar kinds of cults exist; among them are *Vodoun* (origin of the word "voodoo"), which is built around the religious practices of Nigerian and Dahomean tribes; *Ibo*, named after a Nigerian tribe; *Salongo; Juba*, essentially a social dance which once had

[2] Alan P. Merriam, "Songs of the Ketu Cult of Bahia, Brazil," *African Music* I, no. 3 (1956), 54-55.

religious significance, and which was known in the other islands and even in New Orleans; and *Pétro* (which may be named after one of several historical personages named Pedro). Some of these ceremonies are parts of an elaborate ritual cycle known as the Congo-Guinée cycle; all include singing and dancing.

The relationship of the religious material to social dance and song is, in Latin American Negro culture, always a close one, and one that cannot always be explained. Some of the Haitian and Afro-Bahian ceremonial material has lost its religious significance and has become part of the social side of musical life. This is also true of the *Candombe*,[3] a Uruguayan ritual dance performed at the time of the Mardi gras carnival in Montevideo. Here are found certain stock characters—the *gramillero* (an agile young dancer representing a tottering old man), an old Negro woman, a broom-maker, a drummer, and a trophy-bearer. These characters dance in the parade, but it is likely that they represent figures from the earlier time of slavery and the period after emancipation, when African cults and tribal rivalries dominated the life of the urban Negro community. It is interesting to find, also, that the musical style of the Negroes of South America varies according to their location in city or country. Thus, we have said that it is the urban Negroes in Brazil and Uruguay who have held on to the African tradition more than their counterparts in rural areas. But in Surinam, the city Negroes use music with a less African style than do the so-called "bush Negroes" who live in tightly knit communities with little outside influence from white or East Indian inhabitants of the country. In each case, however, it appears that ceremonial material (the music associated with the African-derived cults) has preserved more of the African character than has the music of secular and social provenience. The religious material is, in many cases, hardly to be distinguished from some of the music of West Africa. Rhythms, drum technique, and structure are essentially the same. There is, however, a tendency to use longer, strophic melodies than are usual in West Africa; and the scales, where they did not already conform rather closely to those typical of European music, seem to have been changed in that direction.

[3] Paulo de Carvalho Neto, "The Candombe," *Ethnomusicology* VII (1963), 164-74.

The social structure of the Afro-American cults is a fascinating chapter in the study of the cultural context of traditional music. In the Afro-Bahian cults,[4] there are both priests and priestesses, but most of the initiates are women. At the public performances of the cults' songs and dances, rhythmic accompaniment is produced by various kinds of rattles and bells as well as by hand-clapping. But most important are the drums.

Drummers have a very high and exalted position. They are musicians par excellence. According to Herskovits, the master drummer "moves about the scene, confident, respected. . . . Relaxed, the drum between his legs, he allows the complex rhythm to flow from his sure, agile fingers. It is he who brings on possession through his manipulation of these rhythmic intricacies, yet he himself never becomes possessed."[5] Each cult house has its own master drummer (master drummers are also persons of great prestige in West Africa), who has an important place in the hierarchy of cult leadership. Singing has a somewhat lower value than does drumming. But music is essential to the worship of the deities, for it is through song that they are invoked to participate in the ceremonies. Drums are never played by women, but women do sing and function as leaders of song.

In the Afro-Bahian cults and, typically, in other Afro-American cult groups, drums are played in groups of three; sometimes an iron gong replaces one drum. Each of the two smaller drums usually repeats a single rhythm, while the largest and lowest varies its beats, producing some of the complex and intensely exciting rhythms typical of the Afro-American styles. The drums are played either by hand or with drum sticks. And the making of a drum is itself a complex ritual in which the drum receives its power to communicate with the deities.

While the ceremonial music of the Negro communities of Latin America and the Caribbean is its most prominent—and stylistically most African—musical expression, we must not forget that other kinds of music are also produced. There are work songs, social dance songs, narrative songs of sorts, love songs. The calypso, which presumably originated in Trinidad and spread rapidly throughout the Caribbean, is a unique kind of satirical song (but there are satirical

[4] Melville J. Herskovits, "Drums and Drummers in Afro-Brazilian Cult Life," *Musical Quarterly* XXX (1944), 477-80.

[5] Herskovits, "Drums and Drummers in Afro-Brazilian Cult Life," p. 477.

songs in Africa) that grew out of the racial tensions present in the island and is musically a combination of African, North American Negro, and Spanish popular styles. Jamaican Negroes sing spirituals and sea shanties whose words are of English and North American origin, but which preserve the call-and-response pattern of the African tradition which may have been reinforced by the existence of similar forms in the English sea shanties.

The musical styles of the cult music of Bahia, Haiti, and some of the other Caribbean islands are essentially similar. Call-and-response patterns are dominant. The leader or solo singer may be a woman or a man, but the chorus is usually composed of women. The chorus sings in monophonic fashion, but occasionally individual singers deviate from the main melodic line. Sometimes soloist and chorus overlap. Beneath the vocal line is the all-important rhythm of the drums, each cult, dance, ceremony, or deity having its characteristic rhythms on the basis of which the drummers improvise. The meters are most commonly duple, but sometimes triple, and once a pattern is established it is usually adhered to without much deviation. The scales are most commonly pentatonic without half tones. Tempo varies considerably, but in many of the songs there is gradual acceleration. Nor are the ranges of the melodies uniform; for example, the *Gêgê* cult of Bahia has songs with wide range (most with more than an octave), while those of the *Jesha* cult in the same area average less than an octave. The melodic contours are generally descending, but frequent pendulum-like movements are also characteristic. Melodic intervals are frequently quite large. The form, within the framework of the solo-chorus alternation, is frequently based on the repetition, with some variations, of a single phrase. The soloist is likely to present a theme with variations as the basis of his tune. Leader and chorus sometimes use the same tune, sometimes related ones, and sometimes completely unrelated materials. Occasionally the chorus uses a section (usually a latter or the last) of the soloist's line. Example 9-1 illustrates the songs of the Afro-Bahian cults.

New World Negro instruments

A great many instruments that are at least partly of African origin are used by the Afro-American communities of Latin America. For example, in Haiti certain drums are made of hollow logs. Normally they have single heads and are cylindrical in shape. Height varies from six feet to eighteen inches. Among the idiophones, the *ogan*, a kind of iron bell struck with an external clapper, is promi-

EXAMPLE 9-1. Brazilian Gêgê cult song, from Alan P. Merriam, "Songs of the Gêgê and Jesha Cults," *Jahrbuch für musikalische Volks-und Völkerkunde* I, ed. Fritz Bose (Berlin: Walter de Gruyter & Co., 1963), 122.

nent, as are gourd rattles. Double-headed drums are also used, and so are shallow, single-headed, open drums similar to a tambourine. Various kinds of sticks are used to beat the drums, each cult having its own type of drum sticks and combination of drums. The mosquito drum, a type of musical bow, of which one end is attached to the ground while from the other extends a string attached to a piece of skin covering a hole in the ground, is used as an accompaniment to singing. In this instrument, the hole in the ground functions as resonance chamber, much as the calabash or the player's mouth adds resonance to the sound of musical bows in Southern and Central Africa.

Stamping tubes, hollow tubes struck on the ground or on a board, provide another kind of rhythmic accompaniment. A rather large and deep-sounding version of the African *sansa* or *mbira* (called *marimba* in Haiti) is also found in the Caribbean. Horns and trumpets made of bamboo, each capable of playing only one pitch, are used, as are cow's horns, conch-shell trumpets, and horns improvised from various objects such as phonograph loudspeaker horns. The *clavés*, short sticks made of hardwood and struck together with the use of one hand, are important in the Caribbean. The xylophone, common in Africa, is not as widespread in the Afro-American cultures but does seem to have become one of the important instruments of Central America. In Guatemala, the marimba (xylophone with gourd resonators) has become a national instrument. Throughout the area under discussion the Negro community has brought instruments directly from Africa, has adapted Western materials and technology to the needs of African instruments, and has exerted the African cultural influence by its interest in instruments and instrumental music and its creation of many types, as well as by the prestige and ritual significance that it has placed on the instruments themselves and on the instrumentalists.

The steel drum, an instrument invented in Trinidad during or after World War II, is a fascinating example of the results of the acculturation of African practices in modern Western civilization. Steel oil containers, abandoned and available, their tops hammered into shapes producing the desired scales, were combined into groups of three or four different sizes and accompanied rhythmically by

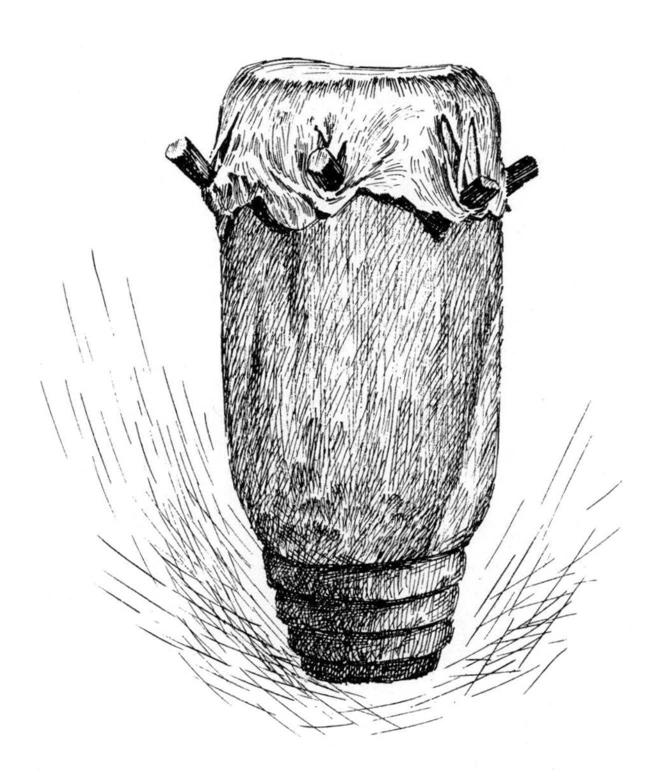

Drum type common in West Africa and the Caribbean.

idiophones—rattles, clavés, or bells. The bottom sections of the containers were cut off later, and the steel drums were placed on special stands. Each "drum" is capable of playing simple melodic material. The result is music of a strongly rhythmic character, with polyphony of an ostinato nature, and with each "drum" (or "pan," as they are called by the players) having a particular musical function, as in a jazz band.

Aside from African-derived and especially invented instruments, Western instruments such as the guitar and banjo (which may have been developed on the basis of African influences) are widely used in the Negro communities of Latin America and the Caribbean. (Negro instruments in North America are mentioned in the next section.)

Negro folk music in the United States

The musical development of the Negroes in North America, and especially in the United States, has been rather different from that of other New World Negroes. Rather than living in relatively closed communities in which African tribal groups could still function, the U.S. Negroes were brought from the West Indies, where aspects of African culture had already begun to change or to disappear, and lived in close contact with their white masters. While the survival of the West African religious cults was to some extent assured in Latin America because of the similarity of some aspects of Roman Catholicism, the impact of the Protestant denominations in the U.S. was of such a nature as to annihilate most of the West African religious practices. Nevertheless, the U.S. Negroes retained much of the value structure of the African heritage, and while their folk music does not sound African in the sense that the music of Haiti and Bahia does, it contains some African stylistic features. More important, the independent developments in American Negro music are frequently the result of African musical values. Thus, the call-and-response patterns are not found too frequently in American Negro folk song; but the original importance of this form—essentially a kind of alternation, dividing up a tune between leader and chorus, with a sanctioning of improvisation—seems possibly to have

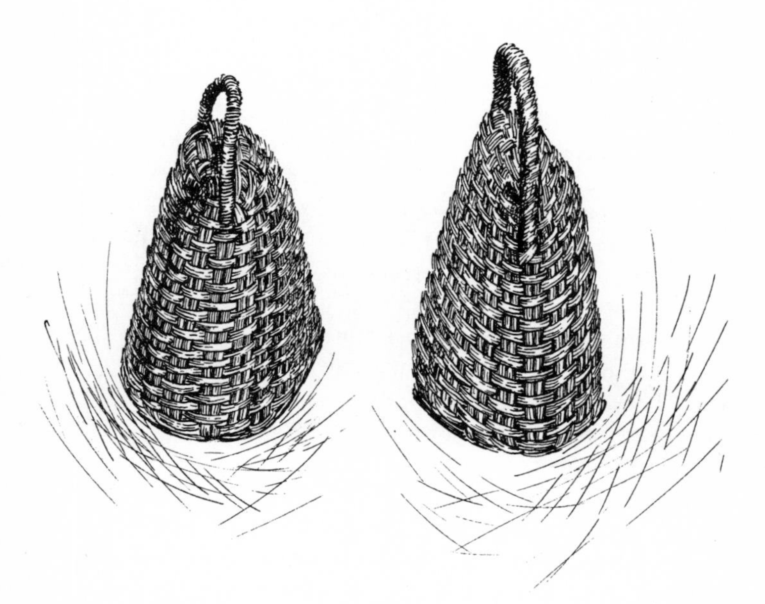

Basket rattles, as found in Haiti or West Africa.

led to the alternation of the various instruments for the "choruses" in jazz.

The importance of rhythm became a part of the American Negro tradition, even though the specific rhythmic sounds of Africa, on the whole, did not. Again, the occasional preference for throaty and rasping singing (found also in the Caribbean) is probably traceable to certain West African singing which sometimes makes use of yodeling and imitating of instruments and animal sounds.

As in Africa, instruments play a large role in U.S. Negro folk music, larger than in the North American white culture. Many of these instruments are European-derived (mouth organ, banjo, fiddles, brass instruments) while others are actually derived from African models or fashioned in order to produce the sounds made on African instruments. In the former category are several that are hardly found today but are reported to have been present in the United States in the nineteenth century and earlier: the *sansa*, hollowed log drums, and gourd rattles. In the latter category we find the washtub or gutbucket, related to the musical bow and to the Haitian mosquito drum; washboards used as scrapers and placed on baskets for resonance; frying pans, cowbells, bottles, wood or bone clappers. These are instruments that are not genetically related to African forms, but they seem to have been invented or improvised to produce African-like sounds.

There are reports of the southern scene by nineteenth-century American observers regarding the existence of musical practices, such as Afro-American cults, similar to those that can be observed in twentieth-century Brazil and the Caribbean. But by the twentieth century, North American Negro music seems to have lost these practices and become much more dominated by the influence of the American whites. Thus, the type of folk song most closely associated with the U.S. Negro, the spiritual, is to a large extent a borrowing from the rural southern whites.[6] The songs sung by the Negroes are frequently identical in text and melodic content with the so-called "white spirituals" sung in the southern mountain regions. But they are sung in a different manner—with more rhythmic accompaniment, call-and-response forms, and improvisation. Parentheti-

[6] D. K. Wilgus, *Anglo-American Folksong Scholarship Since 1898* (New Brunswick, N.J.: Rutgers University Press, 1959), p. 344-64.

cally, we should say that the question of the origin and development of the Negro spiritual's style has not been answered in a satisfactory way, for the white spirituals are also frequently sung in a very vigorous and rhythmically un-hymn-like way—whether through Negro influence or not, we don't know.

George Pullen Jackson (1874-1953)[7] assembled a large number of parallels between Negro and white spirituals. These are taken largely from nineteenth-century collections; and while the tunes of the songs are presented, we have no information about the style of singing used in these early notations. Nevertheless, Example 9-2 shows one tune used as both a white and a Negro spiritual; it is the famous "Swing Low, Sweet Chariot," which is similar in melodic content to a white American hymn tune entitled "Gaines."

The United States Negroes have many other kinds of folk songs: work songs, love songs, ballads, children's songs and lullabies, and so forth. Many of these are simply taken over from the heritage of the whites, and some, though originated by Negroes, are nevertheless patterned after the music of the Anglo-American community. The Negro tradition has always been influenced by the whites, and much of the basic material in it is essentially of European origin; only in the style of performance can we detect definitely African roots. One exception to this tendency is the blues, a type of song best described as a lament.

Possibly the blues are related to those spirituals which, as a sign of protest and of discontent, identify the American Negroes with the Jews in Egyptian slavery. The term "blues" actually applies to songs with many different forms. The so-called field blues are simply short calls and wails, frequently with indefinite pitch, repeated several times, perhaps originally by field hands in the cotton fields communicating with each other; sometimes they are sung alternately by two persons. As in Africa, the Negroes in the United States have developed individual song makers who composed or improvised songs, or who created material out of songs already in existence, and who became masters recognized by the community. These are presumably the individuals who created new songs in the Western style.

Probably the most famous of these U.S. Negro singers was

[7] George Pullen Jackson, *White and Negro Spirituals* (New York: J. J. Augustin, 1943); also his *White Spirituals in the Southern Uplands* (New York: J. J. Augustin, 1933).

EXAMPLE 9-2. Negro spiritual, "Swing Low, Sweet Chariot," and analogous white spiritual, from George Pullen Jackson, *White and Negro Spirituals* (New York: J. J. Augustin, 1943), pp. 182-83.

Lead Belly, whose real name was Huddie Ledbetter, a Texas convict who was discovered by the famous folk song collector, John Lomax. Lead Belly sang many songs, but perhaps his main contribution was a number of blues songs. Typically the form of these was also adopted by the early jazz bands that played blues. It consists of three parts, the first two similar in content (both musically and textually), while the third contrasts. This form can be observed in such well-known blues as the "St. Louis Blues," but also in Lead Belly's songs, such as "Shorty George" and "Fort Worth and Dallas Blues." Other types of blues songs have different forms, some of them based essentially on one musical phrase. Thus, Example 9-3, "Now Your Man Done Gone," collected in Alabama, is essentially a descending set of variations on the first phrase. Typically, Negro songs use fewer different melodic phrases than do the songs of the American whites—another possible survival of African styles.

EXAMPLE 9-3. U.S. Negro folk song, "Now your man done gone," collected in Alabama, from Harold Courlander, *Negro Folk Songs from Alabama* (New York: Wenner-Gren Foundation for Anthropological Research, 1960), p. 52.

A frequently mentioned characteristic of U.S. Negro songs is the so-called "blue note," the flatted or slightly lowered third and seventh degrees in a major scale. The origin of this phenomenon is not known, but it probably cannot be traced to Africa. Here is a musical trait which may, possibly, have come into folk music from the practices of American Negro popular and jazz musicians.

Another group of North American Negro songs that is quite distinct from its counterpart among the whites is the counting-out rimes and other children's game songs and rimes. These, again, are performed with mannerisms perhaps derived from Africa, with strict adherence to metric patterns, some rhythmic complexity such as syncopation, and the undeviating tempo typical also of West Africa and perhaps resulting from the "metronome sense" described in Chapter 7. These rimes, of which the popular "I asked my mother for fifty cents" and "Head-shoulder baby" are examples, are sometimes sung, sometimes spoken. The call-and-response technique is often used. Interestingly, they are heard frequently in the Negro areas of northern cities as well as in the South.

A further category of Negro song to be mentioned is the work song. Here again, traces of the African heritage show up. Work songs—songs actually sung while working, and with rhythms related to those of the work being done—are not common in the Western European tradition (sea shanties are an important exception). But work songs have been found in African Negro music, and perhaps their existence in Africa contributed to their development in the American Negro community. Their style is, of course, not at all African. Some of the work songs, such as "Pick a Bale of Cotton," actually deal with the work. Others, such as Lead Belly's "Elnora," are simply a group of words, euphonious but hardly related to the job, which supply a pleasant and rhythmic accompaniment to labor such as wood-cutting. This song type has stimulated trained American composers such as George Gershwin and Jerome Kern ("Ole Man River") as much as any kind of Negro song.

The use of the voice by American Negro folk singers is often traceable to African singing styles. The much more relaxed, open way of singing, sometimes varied by the use of purposely raucous and harsh notes, is rather similar to some African singing and quite different from the rather tense and restrained manner of singing among southern whites; yet it is probably in no way biologically determined.

Most of the heritage of the United States Negroes is found in the South. The northern Negro communities that have existed for some time have become, essentially, members of the Anglo-American musical community and look down on the recent immigrants from the South as being steeped in superstition and rural tradition. Yet even in the northern cities it is still possible to find musical culture—in churches, on playgrounds, and in the bars of slum areas—that shows its dependence on the African background, and which keeps the folk music of the American Negroes to some extent a heritage objectively different from that of their white compatriots.

Bibliography and discography

Two publications by Richard A. Waterman provide theoretical background for the study of New World Negro music: " 'Hot' Rhythm in Negro Music," *Journal of the American Musicological Society*, I (1948), 24-37, and "African Influence on American Negro Music," in *Acculturation in the Americas*, ed. Sol Tax (Chicago: University of Chicago Press, 1952). Several studies of South American Negro music are important reading: Alan P. Merriam, "Songs of the Ketu Cult of Bahia, Brazil," *African Music*, I (1956), 53-82; Melville J. Herskovts, "Drums and Drummers in Afro-Brazilian Cult Life," *Musical Quarterly*, XXX (1944), 447-92; Luis Felipe Ramon y Rivera, "Rhythmic and Melodic Elements in Negro Music of Venezuela," *J-IFMC*, XIV (1962), 56-60; and Mieczyslaw Kolinski, "Part III, Music" in *Suriname Folklore* by M. J. and Frances Herskovits (New York: J. J. Augustin, 1936).

Negro music in the Caribbean is discussed, with musical transcriptions, in Harold Courlander, *The Drum and the Hoe* (Berkeley: University of California Press, 1960), a study of Haitian voodoo culture. Peter Seeger, "The Steel Drum: a New Folk Instrument," *Journal of American Folklore*, LXXI (1958), 52-57, presents a recent development. Among the numerous publications on U.S. Negro music, John and Alan Lomax, *Negro Folk Songs as Sung by Lead Belly* (New York: Macmillan, 1936), George Pullen Jackson, *White and Negro Spirituals* (New York: J. J. Augustin, 1943) and Harold Courlander, *Negro Folk Music U.S.A.* (New York: Columbia University Press, 1963) are landmarks because of their theoretical importance.

Important records of Negro music in Latin America are *Music of Haiti*, collected by Harold Courlander, Folkways P 403, 407, 432 (3 disks); *Cult Music of Trinidad*, Folkways 4478; and *Afro-Bahian Religious Songs of Brazil*, Library of Congress AAFS 61-65, Album 13 (78 rpm records). Among the numerous recordings of North American Negro music we mention two large sets of records, *Music from the South*, recorded by Frederic Ramsey, Folkways FP 650-58 (9 disks) and *Southern Folk Heritage Series*, edited by Alan Lomax, Atlantic 1346-52 (7 disks, including white and Negro music). Also worth mentioning are *Leadbelly's Last Sessions*, Folkways FP 241-42 (4 disks) and *The Rural Blues*, edited by Samuel B. Charters, RFB Records RF 202 (2 disks).

10

Western and Western-Descended Folk Music in the Americas

The predominant cultural characteristics of the Americas were imported from various European countries, mainly Great Britain and the Hispanic peninsula. Some of them were retained in their old forms, some continued to develop and changed to forms quite different from those of the old countries, and some of course were spiced with elements of the Negro and Indian cultures also found in the New World. In music, too, we find ancient European forms preserved, but we also find European forms that have changed in peculiarly American ways, and we find the preservation of European forms to have been selective—those aspects which fit the American culture that happens to be involved may be kept, while others may not. Moreover, we can observe the various national European forms combining with each other and with the Indian and Negro traditions.

South American folk music

Latin American folk music, on the whole, has less of the old Hispanic heritage preserved in it than North American folk music has of the British tradition. Of course there is variation among nations in this respect. For example, Bolivia, which has a population largely of Indian descent, has a good deal of folk music with Spanish words and tunes using Indian instruments and accompanying dances of Indian origin. Argentina, with its population largely of European origin, may actually have preserved some medieval Spanish tunes. Cuba, of which a large segment of the population is of partially African descent, has developed a musical style with a mixture of Spanish and African stylistic traits. Brazilian folk music is much influenced by its Afro-American element. Colombia, which has essentially a very conservative cultural tradition and is geographically isolated by mountains and tropical forest, has preserved some of the oldest Spanish material known in the New World.

Again, as in the transfer of African material to the Americas, syncretism accounts for the creation of certain forms and the preservation of others. Thus, the development of characteristic and memorable rhythms that became the basis of Latin American popular dances—the rumba, samba, and conga—was probably made possible by the fact that both the West African and the Hispanic traditions favored complicated, driving rhythms with steady, pulsating patterns. The combination of stylistic elements from the Indian and Spanish populations of Bolivia and Peru (which did not occur between the English and Indian styles in North America) was probably in part due to the greater musical sophistication of the Peruvian and Bolivian populations as compared to the relatively simpler musical cultures of the North American Indians.

The Latin American folk music scene is, then, a complex one, and we are again obliged to resort to a few examples of what is found rather than to try to survey in a few pages the entire wealth of song, dance, and instrument types.

Argentina is a good example of a region that has preserved its Spanish heritage. For example, we find there a multitude of *tonadas*, songs of a type derived from the old Spanish *romance*. The Spanish *jota* was once extremely popular in Argentine cities. The *cifra* is a song type whose text consists of questions and answers, and which sometimes has antiphonal musical structure with guitar interludes between vocal sections. And there are numerous folk and popular dances of Spanish origin. At the same time, the Argentines seem to have been selective in their choice of Spanish material to be preserved. Thus they do not have many songs that make use of the presumably Arabic-derived, nonmetrical, ornamented style in Spanish singing; rather, they use the evidently more recent style of Spanish folk music, the style that has lively rhythms, polyphony in parallel thirds or sixths, and a pronounced affection for triple meter. The Spanish *romance*, itself, and the *cante hondo* or *flamenco* did not become important in Argentine folk music. Thus we have an essentially Hispanic folk music culture; but there are, nevertheless, dance types derived at least partially from the Indian culture in Argentina. The latter is true to an even greater degree in Chile, a nation which, though geographically in a position somewhat similar to that of Argentina, has a body of folklore more influenced by the Indians.

Argentine folk music has also been influenced to a large extent by the many immigrants from countries other than Spain. Thus it is possible to collect German folk songs, and the large Italian-descended population may be responsible for the tendency of Argentine folk music to consist largely of the rhythmic and sometimes operatic-sounding songs from the Spanish folk repertory. Uruguayan folk music is relatively similar to that of Argentina.

Bolivia and Peru are good examples of nations in which the Spanish culture was very much influenced by that of the Indians. Thus, even their Spanish-speaking villages have a kind of traditional music that has elements of Indian musical culture. The widespread use of panpipes, aboriginally an Indian instrument, is an example. Indian end-blown flutes are used in conjunction with European types of drums in processions for Catholic saints. It is very difficult, in Peru, Bolivia, and Ecuador, to separate the musical elements of Indian origin from those of the European tradition. Acculturation began in the sixteenth century and was consciously fostered by the Catholic missionaries who realized that the survival of Catholicism depended in part on its absorption of native elements (our theory of syncretism again). The elements of the two cultures combined to form inseparable units. Essentially, the tunes are European in style, but they are tunes that have a great deal of repetition and which use scales with five tones or fewer. The instruments are frequently of Indian origin, as is the style of the percussion accompaniment.

This kind of arrangement of traits seems to be the basis of the musical style of the *Chunchus and Quollas* dance of Peru. A dramatic dance, it represents incidents from the period of conquest. Two sides, representing Spanish and Indian soldiers, appear; and there are individual characters such as the Fair Imilla, an Indian who betrays her people, danced by soloists. Much of the folk music of Peru, Bolivia, and Ecuador is accompaniment to dances, most of which have Indian names.

The special character of Brazilian folk music is due to the importance of the Negro population in much of Brazilian culture. Not only do the Negro communities have their own traditions, which, as we indicated in Chapter 9, sometimes revolve around styles that are still very close to Africa. The folk music of the Brazilian whites is also influenced by African music, especially by the driving rhythms and the importance of percussion instruments. Thus, for instance, the figure ♫♪♩ ♪, common in Spain and Portugal, seems to have been changed in Brazil to the syncopated rhythm, ♬ ♪ ♫. In addition to the Negro tradition, the music of the Catholic church, especially Gregorian chant, is thought to have played a role in the development of Brazilian folk music. Again, Brazil has a large number of distinct folk dance forms: *batuque*, *samba*, *jongo*, *maxixe*, *cururu* and *fandango* are the most prominent. The *samba*, best known of the Brazilian popular dances, was originally a round dance. In addition to the social dances there are popular dramatic dances in which events from the history of Brazil and Portugal are acted in pantomime; some of these are rather similar to the *candombe* of the Uruguayan Negroes described in Chapter 9.

Middle America: Mexico and the Caribbean

Mexican folk music is largely in the Spanish tradition, and while the Mexican Indians retain to some extent their native musical styles, there seems to have been less influence of the Indian styles on the Spanish-derived folk music here than in Bolivia, Peru, and Ecuador (which have a comparably large Indian population). A tremendous number of Mexican songs and song types has been collected. For example, the *corrido*, a narrative song type derived from the Spanish *romance*, with a four-line stanza but with repetitive melodic structure, exists in various regional types. *Corridos* often deal with current events, crimes, and love stories, much as the English broadside ballads tell of sensational happenings, and new ones are still coming into existence. Songs from the fine art tradition are also sometimes reshaped into the form of the *corrido* by the folk tradition.

One difference between Spanish and Latin American folk music in general is the importance of instruments in the latter. The presence of instrumental refrains or ritornellos (*tornadas*) between phrases and stanzas has caused the melodies sometimes to assume asymmetrical form. The frequent use of 6/8 meter in Spanish folk song is, analogously, sometimes relieved, in Mexican folk music, by 5/8 or 7/8 measures.

An interesting manifestation of the instrument culture in Mexico is the development of *mariachi* orchestras—groups of three to a dozen players of string instruments (violins, guitars, mandolins, double basses) that play traditional and popular tunes in city streets. In recent decades, brass instruments have been added to these *mariachi* orchestras, whose name, by the way, is evidently derived from the French *mariage* because they were once frequently utilized at weddings.

The early missionaries in Mexico evidently tried hard to suppress the native Indian musical culture. They did not succeed entirely, but as a result of their work much of the folk music of the Hispanic tradition has evidently found its way into the culture of some Mexican Indian groups. Vicente Mendoza,[1] a great authority on Mexican folk music, presents songs of the Otomí Indians of Northern Mexico that show the characteristic triplets of Spanish folk song, and which have elements of major tonality emphasizing tonic and third. Other Otomí songs give even greater evidence of European influence—parallel thirds and sixths, something hardly to be found in aboriginal Indian music. But these songs are probably not simply Spanish songs sung by Indians; their style would be exceedingly simple for Spain, for they typically have short melodies,

[1] For example, see Vicente T. Mendoza, "Musica indigena Otomí," *Revista de Estudios Musicales* II, No. 5-6 (1950-1951), 527.

few tones, and small range. More likely they are songs composed by the Indians, who were still steeped in the Indian tradition but who had had some contact with Hispanic folk music in Mexico.

The problem of the origin of Hispanic tunes in Latin American folk music is generally unsolved. But we can say with some certainty that the tunes sung in Latin America are for the most part not simply imports from Spain and Portugal (while the words more frequently are). They are more usually songs either composed in Latin America in the styles brought from Europe, or they are indeed songs brought from Europe centuries ago but so changed by the process of oral tradition that the tunes in Europe that are related to them can no longer be recognized as relatives; or perhaps it is the European tunes that have undergone change. This situation is not completely paralleled by the traditions of minority groups living in South America—Germans, East Europeans, Italians—for these have preserved many of the songs that they brought from Europe, but they have not to a large extent created new material in the traditional styles. Example 10-1, Mexican folk music, illustrates a few (but, of course, omitting a multitude) of the characteristics of Hispanic folk music in Latin America.

EXAMPLE 10-1. Mexican polyphonic folk song, from Vicente T. Mendoza, *La Canción Mexicana* (Mexico, D.F.: Instituto de Investigaciones Esteticas, Universidad Nacional Autonoma de Mexico, 1961), p. 239.

Incidentally, among the important European forms of song and dance used by the Spanish-speaking Latin Americans are a good many that are not of Hispanic origin. Thus the mazurka (of Polish origin), the polka (Czech), the waltz, the polonaise, even the minuet and the gavotte-like *cuando* are among the dances of the Latin American rural population.

But the changes that Spanish music has undergone and the complete fusion of African and Hispanic styles that can occur are best seen in the music of Cuba, which was a Spanish possession longer than any other American land. Thus, the *bolero*, in triple meter in Spain, was changed in Cuba to a dance in duple meter with characteristic syncopation. A typical 6/8 metric arrangement of Spanish music, alternating between 6/8 and 3/4 (hemiola), was preserved in Cuba, but elaborated to a duple meter figure with syncopation, ♩ ♬♩ ♬♩ or ♩. ♩. ♩, which subsequently became prominent in jazz.

Among the most interesting survivals of Spanish folk music in the Americas is the music of the religious folk plays of Mexico and the southwestern United States. Performed mainly by Indians, these plays are descendants of the liturgical dramas—mystery and morality plays—of the Middle Ages. They are called *autos* and deal with Biblical stories such as that of Cain and Abel, the Nativity, and the Passion of Christ. Most of the dialogue is spoken, but songs, called *letras*, appear at certain points and are sung by the congregation. The style of these songs is derived from Spanish folk music. It is slow, measured, and usually in the major or harmonic minor modes, and it is evidently related to the style of the *romances* and other narrative folk songs.

Ethnic minorities in North America

Consideration of an important tradition of Spanish-American folk music in the United States also leads us to mention the existence of other folk music styles that flourish in North America and which were brought from various European countries. As we have indicated, such imported traditions currently alive among minority groups must be numerous in Latin America, but those of the United States are better known and have been studied in more detail. In many cultures, religious and ceremonial life tends to attract the most conservative elements, and the most archaic aspects of a tradition are usually to be found in its religious manifestations. Thus, perhaps, the oldest European folk music preserved in the Americas may be that which is associated with religion. The Spanish liturgical dramas are one example; another is the tradition of German spiritual folk song which is found especially in Pennsylvania but also among the Amish of the midwestern United States.

The Amish are a religious community related to the Mennonites. Of Swiss and German origin, they began leaving Germany in the seventeenth century, some migrating first to Russia and then, in the early nineteenth century, to the United States, while others came directly to America. Their austere manner of living and their conservative traditions kept them essentially out of contact with other German-Americans. Devoting themselves exclusively to farming, they use music only for worship. Their hymns are of two types, an older one that is possibly a survival of a medieval hymn-singing tradition, and a newer one evidently part of the German-American spiritual tradition of Pennsylvania.

To most listeners, the older hymns of the Amish scarcely sound like a product of Western musical culture. They are monophonic and sung without accompaniment, without perceptible meter, with syllables drawn out over many tones, and with slowly executed ornaments. Only when one becomes acquainted with the style does one see in it any resemblance to the hymn tunes of the German reformed churches. This can be done by connecting the first notes of the textual syllables to each other, even when they are short and seemingly insignificant. Since this style of singing is not found in Europe today, how did it come about? Possibly the Amish, after arriving in Russia or the United States, began to slow down the hymns they had sung in Germany, to add ornaments, and to draw out the metric structure until it was not to be recognized. On the other hand, possibly their way of singing was once widely used in the German-speaking rural areas of Europe, and has simply been retained by the Amish in America while it underwent complete change in Europe under the impact of the all-pervading musical influence of the cities and courts. At any rate, the Amish hymns are an example of the marginal survival that characterizes the musical culture of the Americas to the extent that it is derived from Europe.[2]

[2] Bruno Nettl, "The Hymns of the Amish, an Example of Marginal Survival," *Journal of American Folklore* LXX (1957), 327-328.

The newer hymns of the Amish correspond to the spiritual tradition of the Pennsylvania German culture. This culture represents an interesting mixture of German—particularly South German—and British elements, including a special dialect of German that has grown up with certain elements of American English phonology. The songs of the Pennsylvania Germans are in part simply those of the German tradition, and in part based on tunes from the Anglo-American heritage. Thus the so-called Pennsylvania spirituals, folk hymns with German words, are really products of the spiritual revival of the early 1800's, which involved Methodists and Baptists in the English-speaking community, and the influence of Negro music and of Negro spirituals, all converging on the Pennsylvania German community. As a result, the tunes are of various origins: Some are those of secular German folk songs, a few are derived from early German hymns, some come from the white spiritual tradition ("The Battle Hymn of the Republic" appears with several sets of words). The Pennsylvania German spiritual is not, of course, a purely folkloric type of music. Hymn books were printed and professional hymn writers contributed to it. But much of the musical material was and is identical to that which lives in the authentic folk culture; and most of the tunes were, in contrast to the words, actually passed on by oral tradition and were performed at camp meetings without the use of books, and lived by means of variation and communal re-creation.

Just as the German folk culture lives on in the small towns of Eastern Pennsylvania, other Western European traditions can be found thriving in other rural areas of North America. Northern Michigan and Minnesota are repositories of Scandinavian and Finnish folklore. The southern Midwest and Louisiana are the homes of people who still sing, or at any rate can occasionally remember for a collector, the folk songs of France. Of course the eastern part of Canada, especially the province of Quebec, is rich in the folklore of French-Canadians. Much as the United States yields a repertory of English songs at least as large as that of England herself, the French-Canadians sing essentially all of the older French folk songs; and Marius Barbeau, veteran collector of the songs in this tradition, records that for song upon song more variants have been found in America than in France. One group of individuals who particularly carried the French tradition is the *voyageurs*, French Canadians who paddled canoes through the Great Lakes in the fur trade, and who sang for amusement and as a rhythmic accompaniment to paddling. On the whole, the French Canadian songs do not seem to differ greatly from those of France.

Folk music in American cities

The Eastern and Southern European traditions are preserved in the large cosmopolitan cities of the United States. Here, a tendency of minority groups, particularly those which arrived rather recently, to settle in special areas or enclaves, is responsible for the preservation and special development of these traditions. Thus, large collections of Hungarian and Slovak song have been made in Cleveland,[3] Yiddish and Puerto Rican folk music has been studied in New York, and the songs of Poles, Syrians, and many other groups have been recorded in Detroit. In some cases, old songs can be found relatively undisturbed, and the American city acts as the agent of marginal survival. At other times, the European traditions are changed because of the pressures of urban American culture. Thus there seems to be a tendency to favor dance and instrumental music over other types; perhaps this is due to the fact that young Americans of foreign descent have less of an interest in the words of the songs, which they may not even understand, than in the tunes. Organized teaching of folk songs, even from song books, by members of the ethnic group who are noted for their knowledge may be one way of preserving the material. Group singing is more prominent than in the European parent traditions. Singing clubs and dance groups are formed in order to keep the tradition alive, for music and dance play an important part in keeping an ethnic group in a city from losing its identity.

Furthermore, the musical style of Eastern European folk songs sung in the American cities may change, for those songs which come closest to being acceptable in terms of the American popular tune tradition are those which are preserved by the ethnic groups. The younger individuals in these communities, who by the middle of the twentieth century were no longer able to speak the languages of their grandparents, are stimulated by the appearance of professional

[3] Stephen Erdely, "Folksinging of the American Hungarians in Cleveland," *Ethnomusicology* VIII (1964), 14-27.

dance and instrumental groups from Europe who give concerts on American stages. The original functions of the folk songs on the whole have disappeared in the American city, and the music must serve mainly as entertainment, as an expression of sentimental feeling, and as accompaniment to dancing. Occasionally, new songs in Polish, Hungarian, Slovak and other languages are created, though in such cases it is usually the setting of new words, which deal with American life, to an old tune. Example 10-2 illustrates a Polish folk song (possibly unchanged in transit) collected in Detroit. On the whole, the ethnic groups in the United States perform the music of the old

EXAMPLE 10-2. Polish folk song, "Cztery Mile za Warszawa" ("It was four miles out of Warsaw"), collected in Detroit. Reprinted from *Merrily We Sing, 105 Polish Folksongs* by Harriet M. Pawlowska by permission of the Wayne State University Press. Copyright 1961.

country, sometimes preserving tunes already forgotten in Europe, but more frequently singing the old tunes in less ornamented, shorter, and frequently impoverished style, often tending to change modal tunes to major or minor, heterometric structure to isometric (but not in Eample 10-2), and unaccompanied tunes to songs with chordal accompaniment or singing in parallel thirds.

To a smaller extent than the non-English-speaking groups, the Anglo-American and Negro communities in the cities also have a folk music tradition, largely because many members of these two groups are recent immigrants from the countryside. This contrasts with the European cities, whose population has been more stable, and where mass media and the institutions of art music have had a longer period of impact. One interesting area of urban folk music in America is the body of songs revolving around the labor movement. These songs are of relatively recent origin, their poets and composers are usually known, and they are normally learned first from songbooks and taught by trained organizers. Some of these songs (the best known is "Joe Hill") did pass into oral tradition and can be considered a special type of folk music. Many of them have words protesting the bad treatment of factory workers, miners, migrant farmers, and minority groups. Others sing the praises of labor organizations. Usually, tunes of older folk songs, hymns, music hall ditties, and minstrel songs are used. Often the words parody songs already in the folk tradition. For example, a song sung during a New York state milk strike in 1939 is a parody of "Pretty Polly," a version of the British ballad of the "Cruel Ship's Carpenter":

Mister farmer, mister farmer, come go along with me (twice)
Come hitch up with the milk trust and we'll keep the system free.
So they followed the milk trust stooges and what did they find? (twice)
Nothing in their pockets and a knife from behind.[4]

The existence of folk music in the Anglo-American population of the cities is, however, largely outside the oral tradition. The awareness and knowledge of folk music on the part of the American city dweller has increased greatly since about 1950. The reason for this change in attitude is, of course, the rise of a folk singing movement mainly on the part of students and, as a result, the creation of folk music as a separate class of music somewhere between that of the folk tradition itself and popular music. Folk music as sung by professional folk singers such as Pete Seeger, Burl Ives, and Harry Belafonte, or by ensembles such as the Lamplighters or the Kingston Trio, has few of the attributes of folk music in oral tradition; thus it should perhaps not form part of this discussion. (The artists mentioned differ greatly in their degree of adherence to folk styles.) Nevertheless, the folk singing movement in the cities is a musical and cultural phenomenon worthy of detailed study. It differs from the

[4] John Greenway, *American Folksongs of Protest* (Philadelphia: University of Pennsylvania Press, 1953), p. 215.

authentic folk tradition mainly because the songs are learned not from friends and family but from books, records (field recordings and professional performances), and trained musicians; because many of the songs are composed especially for city consumption (but this may also have been true of many "real" folk songs when they were first composed); because the performer consciously tries to develop certain idiosyncracies and to repeat them in an identical way each time; and because the style of singing—polyphonic, sometimes with virtuoso accompaniment on banjo, guitar, piano, etc.—may be completely different from the style in which these same songs are sung in the countryside. And an urban folk singer may use several traditions and many languages.

As we pointed out in Chapter 1, it may be possible for a song to be a folk song and not a folk song at the same time; and folk songs sung by professional city concert singers are perhaps no longer folk songs. But the basic material, the content of the songs, is still the same. Incidentally, the influence travels from city to country as well as the other way. The singing of folk songs on radio and television has evidently also affected the rural folk tradition, where instrumental accompaniment, part-singing, the "hillbilly" style, and strict adherence to meter seem to have increased since the 1940's.

The use of folk music by urban musicians is not unique in the United States. Folk songs have been used as agents of music education, as a way of fostering patriotism, and as political, economic, and racial propaganda in Europe as well. In the Soviet Union, songs praising Joseph Stalin (with traditional tunes) were introduced into oral tradition before the 1950's. In Nazi Germany, the singing of German folk songs was obligatory for patriotic organizations. And songbooks for elementary-school use everywhere have contained a large quota of folk music. In the United States, the creation of labor unions, wars of independence and expansion, and the struggle for civil rights were all helped along by the organized teaching and singing, by trained musicians, of appropriate folk songs, which frequently consisted of new words specifically written for this purpose set to traditional tunes. Thus we see that there has been, for some centuries, a sort of adjunct phenomenon to rural folk music tradition in Western civilization—the use of folk songs and folk-like songs, usually with traditional tunes, performed by professional and semiprofessional musicians in the cities.

The rural Anglo-American tradition

In the United States, the development of urban folk song culture is partly a result of the development of a strong folk music tradition in the rural Anglo-American community. We have pointed out the importance of this tradition to the survival of British folk music, and, as in South America, we have noted that British material is often better preserved in the New World than in the Old. Of course, the British folk song tradition has undergone changes in America, influenced by the peculiar course of American history and the development of American culture.

The music of American folk songs is partly composed of British and Irish tunes that are not easily distinguished, individually, from their forms as they are found in the British Isles. Partly it comes from popular song and from broadside ballad tunes. The differences between American and British song are greater in the words than in the music, for the words are much more frequently of American origin (often they are parodies of British songs), embodying the specific events of American history and resulting from particular features of American culture—the frontier, the religious revival of the 1800's, the love of humor and exaggeration, the presence of various ethnic minorities, and the particular occupations (cowboys, miners, Indian fighters, etc.) in which Americans had to engage while building a new country.

Taken as a whole, the style of American folk music in English has more melodies in major, fewer pentatonic tunes, more songs in duple meter, less use of accompaniment, but more use of the drone principle in instrumental accompaniment than has the style of Britain. Like the British tradition, and unlike the Negro and some of the ethnic group styles, it is essentially one of solo singing. Melodies that are obviously of nineteenth-century origin, with a definite implied harmony, are common in America. The words of the English songs in America have also been changed, and Americans have made a special selection of material from the British repertory. Thus, there are more humorous folk songs in the American repertory than in the British. Tall tales and other humorous exaggerations are a typical subject. Folk heroes such as the Negro strong man John Henry, the badman Jesse James, and the Slavic steel worker Joe Magarac abound. Broadside ballads telling of the murders and railroad wrecks of a locality are particularly popular, and songs telling of shipwrecks are a specialty of the populations of Newfoundland, Labrador, and New England. Besides preserving British broadsides, Americans have composed a body of broadsides of their own, especially during the nineteenth and early twentieth centuries. They are more apt to deal with violence and romantic love and less with the supernatural and with battles than are their British counterparts.

Regional differences do, of course, appear in folk singing of the United States. According to Alan Lomax,[5] northern folk singers produce a rather relaxed, open-voiced tone, while southern ones are tenser and "pinched-voiced," and those of the West are a blend of the two. Lomax attributes these differences to deep-seated cultural differences involving the relationship between the sexes, the hardships of frontier life, and the presence of the Negro minority in the South. The fact that dancing was prohibited or at least frowned upon by many religious leaders of early America tended to drive dance music from the British Isles into the background, but it produced a distinctly American type of song, the "playparty song," which accompanies marching and dance-like movements similar to those of some children's group games.[6]

Dancing has, however, played a part in the British-American folk culture, as may be seen from the prominence of the square dance, which is drived from the eighteenth and nineteenth-century quadrilles of European high society. A distinctive American feature is the presence of a "caller," who speaks or sings verses instructing the dancers in the routine required in the execution of the dance.

There is also in the American tradition a large body of instrumental music that is used for dancing, and some of which was at one time also used for marching. As a matter of fact, the earliest jazz bands in New Orleans were brass bands that played marching music for funerals and other processions. But this is part of the Negro tradition that has little to do with that of the white North, where fiddle and fife players played ornamented versions of song tunes as well as

[5] Alan Lomax, *The Folksongs of North America in the English Language* (New York: Doubleday & Company, Inc., 1960), p. 1.

[6] For examples, see S. J. Sackett, "Play-Party Games from Kansas," *Heritage of Kansas* V, No. 3 (Sept. 1961), 5-61.

tunes of popular and art music origin. The main instruments of the American folk tradition are the guitar, the banjo, the mandolin, the dulcimer, the violin, and the mouth organ. The dulcimer appears in various forms, some of them similar to those of the Swedish dulcimer described in Chapter 4. As in Europe, the American string instruments are frequently used for music in which the drone principle somehow appears.

Just as many of the instrumental tunes came from the vocal repertory, many tunes originally played were eventually sung. Again, this is a tendency found also in some European cultures. Example 10-3 is a fiddle tune with words; its large range suggests that it may have originated as an instrumental piece which only later began to be used vocally.

EXAMPLE 10-3. Fiddle tune and song, "Prettiest Little Gal in the County, O," collected in Florida, from Alton C. Morris, *Folksongs of Florida* (Gainesville, Florida: University of Florida Press, 1950), p. 226.

Finally, the Negro influence on the white American folk song tradition has been considerable. It can be felt in the occasional "hot rhythm" of singing and accompaniment, in the development of the so-called hillbilly style, in the tendency to stick to one meter (although many white singers do not do this but sing in the parlando-rubato style), in the use of rhythmic handclapping by white folk audiences, and, of course, in the many Negro songs that have become part of the white repertory. Although we do not always know whether a particular characteristic is of Negro or white origin, we are safe in assuming that the presence of the Negro culture in America is one of the important factors that make Anglo-American folk music distinct from its British counterpart.

The American folk music scene is a fitting one for closing a survey of folk and traditional music in the Western continents, for it shows us many of the things that are typical and interesting in folk music everywhere—the preservation of archaic forms, the creation of new styles under the impact of acculturation, special developments due to particular trends in cultural values, and the growth of a special kind of folk music culture in the modern city.

One of the things that our consideration of folk music in the Americas and, indeed, of folk and traditional music everywhere, has shown is the condition of flux in which the material is constantly found. Change, brought about through intercultural contact and through the creative elements within each society, has evidently been present in even the simplest cultures, and it has increased in rapidity as the world's traditions are thrown into contact and conflict with each other as a result of the accelerating Westernization of the entire planet. Will it be possible for traditional musics to survive and to retain some measure of the distinctiveness which has characterized them in the past? Prognostication is not our task here. But if we consider folk music as merely the product of the rural, unlettered classes, and if we consider "primitive" music as nothing but the product of backward peoples, we are bound to find that the traditions in which we are interested are receding and will eventually disappear. On the other hand, if we can retain an interest in the musical cultures of nations and peoples rather than of a musically professional elite, and if we are willing to bend our definitions of folk and traditional music to include such things as "popular" music, jazz, and urban folk song, we may be in a position to investigate the kind of music which will replace, in its social function, the folk and traditional music of the past and present.

While we must perhaps concede the eventual disappearance of traditional musics in the present sense of the concept, we should not assume that this demise is imminent. For many decades, some collectors have pursued their material with the attitude of a last-minute rescue operation, proclaiming the doom of authentic folklore. And indeed, since traditional music is always changing, something of it must always be disappearing. Nevertheless, each year brings new discoveries of unknown styles, unexplored musical cultures, unexpected instruments, and new distributions of musical types, always requiring changes in theory and reorientation of scholarly thought. As long as this is the state of traditional music, one can hardly claim that it is a dying art.

Bibliography and discography

The developments in collecting and studying American folk song are discussed in D. K. Wilgus, *Anglo-American Folksong Scholarship Since 1898* (New Brunswick, N.J.: Rutgers University Press, 1959). A bibliographic survey of ballads originating in America is Malcolm G. Laws, *Native American Balladry* (Philadelphia: American Folklore Society, 1950). The classic collection of British song in the U.S. is Cecil J. Sharp, *English Folk Songs from the Southern Appalachians* (London: Oxford University Press, 1952, 2 vols.); and a modern collection covering all types of song is Alan Lomax, *The Folk Songs of North America in the English Language* (New York: Doubleday & Company, Inc., 1961). Samuel P. Bayard, *Hill Country Tunes* (Philadelphia: American Folklore Society, 1944) is a collection of instrumental folk music. Charles Seeger, "The Appalachian Dulcimer," *Journal of American Folklore*, LXXI (1958), 40-52 discusses one important American folk instrument.

The role of folk music in entertainment and education is discussed in Sven Eric Molin, "Lead Belly, Burl Ives, and Sam Hinton," *Journal of American Folklore*, LXXI (1958), 58-78; and Charles Seeger, "Folk Music in the Schools of a Highly Industrialized Society," *J-IFMC*, V (1953), 40-44.

Spanish-American folk music is discussed in Eleanor Hague, *Latin American Music, Past and Present* (Santa Ana, Calif.: Fine Arts Press, 1934). An important collection is Vicente T. Mendoza, *La Cancion Mexicana* (Mexico: Universidad Nacional, 1961).

The music of other ethnic groups in America is presented in Marius Barbeau, *Jongleur Songs of Old Quebec* (New Brunswick, N.J.: Rutgers University Press, 1962); Harriet Pawlowska, *Merrily We Sing, 105 Polish Folk Songs* (Detroit: Wayne State University Press, 1961); Bruno Nettl, "The Hyms of the Amish: An Example of Marginal Survival," *Journal of American Folklore*, LXX (1957), 323-28; Stephen Erdely, "Folk-singing of the American Hungarians in Cleveland," *Ethnomusicology*, VIII (1964), 14-27; and Jacob A. Evanson, "Folk Songs of an Industrial City" in *Pennsylvania Songs and Legends*, ed. George Korson (Philadelphia: University of Pennsylvania Press, 1949), which deals with Slovak songs in Pittsburgh.

It is difficult to select a group of recommended records from the multitude available for the European-American folk traditions. For the

U.S., the series *Folk Music of the United States* issued by the Library of Congress is excellent. Especially to be mentioned among these are *Folk Music from Wisconsin*, AAFS L55; *Songs of the Michigan Lumberjacks*, AAFS L56; *Anglo-American Songs and Ballads*, AAFS L12, L14; *Songs and Ballads of the Anthracite Miners*, AAFS L16; and *Sacred Harp Singing*, AAFS L11. Lectures on collecting by John Lomax appear on *The Ballad Hunter*, AAFS L49-53 (5 disks). Fine Canadian collections are *Maritime Folk Songs from the Collection of Helen Creighton*, Folkways FE 4307; *Folk Music from Nova Scotia*, Folkways P 1006 (also edited by Helen Creighton); and *Songs of French Canada*, Folkways FE 4482. Spanish-American material appears on *Music of Peru*, Folkways P 415 and *Traditional Music of Peru*, Folkways FE 4456, as well as *Spanish and Mexican Folk Music of New Mexico*, Folkways P 426. An excellent collection of non-English language songs from the U.S., with detailed notes, is *Lithuanian Folk Songs in the United States*, Folkways P 1009.

Index